# Adjudication in the Construction Industry

A specially commissioned Report

.

# Adjudication in the Construction Industry

**A specially commissioned Report**

## Kate Gordon

Sweet & Maxwell

Kate Gordon has asserted her rights under the Copyright, Designs and Patents Act
1988 to be identified as the author of this work

Published by
Sweet & Maxwell Limited of
100 Avenue Road
London NW3 3PF

www.smlawpub-holborn.co.uk

Printed in Great Britain by Bookcraft (Bath) Ltd.

A CIP catalogue record for this book
is available from the British Library

ISBN 075200 4530

No natural forests were destroyed to make this product,
only natural farmed timber was used and re-planted.

# Contents

# Foreword

The aim of Pt II of the Housing Grants, Construction and Regeneration Act 1996 is ambitious—the elimination of traditional adversarial relationships in the construction industry. This is to be achieved by a new statutory right to refer disputes to adjudication. It is this new right which forms the subject matter of this book. The right to adjudicate had its genesis in Sir Michael Latham's report 'Constructing the Team' published in 1994. It was one of the foremost planks of Sir Michael's proposed reforms aimed at restoring 'Trust and Money' to the construction industry. The cashflow problems of the industry could not, he argued, be improved unless there was a cheap, quick enforcement procedure available allowing parties an effective remedy against a defaulter. Parties would deal with each other fairly and sensibly because they knew that a quick remedy was available against them if they did not.

The aims of adjudication are ambitious but the right to adjudicate is enshrined in a single section in the 1996 Act. This sets out a minimalist framework: a decision must be reached within 28 days of referral; the adjudicator must act impartially, he must have the power to take the initiative in ascertaining the facts and the law and his decision is binding pending final determination of the dispute. It also confers immunity on adjudicators except in the case of bad faith.

The Act clearly leaves a lot unsaid about the new right to adjudicate and this book attempts to fill in the gaps. It looks at the related Statutory Instruments which take effect at the same time as Pt II of the 1996 Act—particularly the Scheme for Construction Contracts (England and Wales) Regulations 1998 (SI No 649) and the Construction Contracts (England and Wales) Exclusion Order 1998 (SI No 648). It draws on experience in related areas of dispute resolution, particularly expert determination and arbitration. Where there is no helpful guide to be found elsewhere, it speculates on the likely approach of the participants, their legal advisers and, ultimately, the courts to this new statutory animal.

There are already those who say that adjudication will generate more disputes than it solves. The mere existence of a cheap and speedy procedure will, they argue, promote disputes and once a decision has gone as far as an adjudicator it will inevitably be appealed to arbitration or litigation by the aggrieved party. They also suggest that adjudicators' awards will never be enforceable, that there will be myriad jurisdictional challenges and that lawyers will inevitably play games with it.

Who knows? It is a brave lawyer who writes about a revolutionary piece of legislation before there is any practical experience of it. All that can be said with certainty is that this book will be an invaluable guide to all of us as we struggle through the early days of adjudication in the construction industry.

Ann Minogue
Cameron McKenna
6 April 1998

# Table of Cases

# Table of Statutes

# Table of Statutory Instruments

# 1

# An Introduction to the Housing Grants, Construction and Regeneration Act 1996, Pt II

## 1.1 The Act

### 1.1.1 Extent of the Act

The Housing Grants, Construction and Regeneration Act 1996 ('the Act') is one of the most revolutionary pieces of legislation ever to apply to the construction industry. It applies not only to contracts for the execution of construction works, but also to contracts for the repair, refurbishment and demolition of buildings, structures and other works, together with contracts for most kinds of professional services associated with construction works. Most companies and individuals operating in the construction industry will be subject to its terms. Many companies and individuals working in industries serving or related to the construction industry will find that the operation of the Act has practical, if not directly applicable legal, ramifications for their business.

Part II of the Act introduces into the law mandatory provisions to govern construction contracts and creates a number of new rights for parties to construction contracts. It is with only one of these rights that this book is concerned; namely, the right to adjudication. Unless the context otherwise requires, reference in this book to the Act should be read as reference to the Act in so far as it relates to adjudication.

### 1.1.2 The structure of s 108

Section 108 of the Act creates the right to refer a dispute arising under a construction contract for adjudication under a procedure complying with that section. If the construction contract makes provision for adjudication in accordance with s 108, the parties are bound by that contractual provision. If it does not make such provision, the Scheme for Construction Contracts ('the Scheme') applies. The Scheme is a statutory code passed by delegated legislation in March 1998 containing, *inter alia*, adjudication rules which apply in default of contractual provision complying with s 108. If the Scheme applies in default of contractual provision complying with s 108, its terms as regards adjudication will apply in their entirety. The parties will have no power (save with mutual consent) to apply certain provisions and disapply others. If the parties are content for the Scheme to apply, they need make no express contractual provision for adjudication. Adjudication as envisaged by s 108 is intended, in the absence of agreement to the contrary, to result in a decision with interim binding effect only, capable of being reversed by some other dispute resolution procedure, such as court or arbitration proceedings.

Section 108 prescribes certain minimum requirements which the contractual adjudication procedure must meet if the Scheme is to be avoided. The contract may make adjudication provision beyond that required by the Act, but must not derogate from the statutory minimum requirements. If it does so, the Scheme applies. The statutory minimum requirements are few and are barely sufficient to create a workable adjudication scheme. For this reason, the parties will usually wish to supplement and expand upon them. Careful drafting of the adjudication provisions of a contract, whether required by the Act or not, will enable the parties to shape the essential nature of their contractual adjudication scheme and to maximise the benefit and minimise the burden of the right and obligation to adjudicate.

### 1.1.3   The nature of adjudication under the Act

The adjudication mechanism embodied within the Act is intended to be swift once it has been commenced. From beginning to end the procedure should not exceed 35 days, which period may be extended only in limited circumstances. There are no rules governing procedure or evidence and the adjudicator is entitled to take an investigative approach to his task. In the absence of contractual provision to the contrary, the adjudicator is not required to give reasons for his decision which is binding only until such time as it is overturned in court or arbitration proceedings. In many respects the adjudication procedure differs radically from the procedures adopted in either court or arbitration.

### 1.1.4   Adjudication as a right and obligation

Adjudication is a right. The Act does not require a claimant to seek the resolution of his dispute by adjudication—he is free to go to court or arbitration if he prefers. He is free to go to court or arbitration *and* adjudication if he wishes—there is no restriction upon the concurrency of proceedings. Adjudication is also an obligation. A person against whom adjudication is sought has no effective choice but to defend the proceedings, the result of which will bind him whether he participates in them or not.

## 1.2   History and policy of the Act

### 1.2.1   The Latham Report

The genesis of the provisions of Pt II of the Act lies in the final report of Sir Michael

Latham, issued in July 1994, and entitled *Constructing the Team* ('the Latham Report'). The Latham Report was commissioned to undertake a wide ranging review of the construction industry. Latham's terms of reference were to consider current procurement and contractual arrangements and current roles, responsibilities and performance of the participants, including the client, with particular reference to a number of factors, including contractual issues and methods of dispute resolution. The Latham Report was issued following extensive industry-wide consultation. The Latham Report concludes that 'adjudication should be the normal method of dispute resolution'.[1]

When the Latham Report was issued, it was greeted with enthusiasm throughout the construction industry. Sir Michael's recommendations on adjudication were welcomed as a possible means of overcoming the ills besetting the construction industry, such as adversarial attitudes and poor cash flow. The Latham Report recommended that a system of adjudication should be introduced within all standard forms of contract and that this 'should be underpinned by legislation'.[2] The Act is that underpinning legislation.

### 1.2.2 Objectives of adjudication under the Act

This book is not the place for a critical analysis of the objectives of the Latham Report or the Act. In a number of significant respects, the Act does not follow the recommendations of the Latham Report. Notwithstanding, a brief summary of the objectives of the Act, as ascertained from the parliamentary debates preceding the passing of the Act, should set in context the substantive provisions of the Act and provide some indication as to how they are likely to be construed. The objectives of the Act include the:
(a) reversal of the claims-oriented attitudes prevalent in the construction industry;
(b) reduction in costs expended by the industry in the resolution of disputes;
(c) improvement in cash flow, and;
(d) prevention of unresolved disputes holding up work on site.
To this end, the Act provides a swift, hopefully cheap and temporarily binding procedure for rendering decisions in relation to disputes arising during the currency of, and indeed after, the completion of a project.

### 1.2.3 Are these objectives likely to be achieved?

Only when the Act has been in force for long enough to allow the effect of the adjudication provisions to be evaluated on an empirical basis can it be said whether adjudication has achieved its objectives. All that can be done at present is to speculate upon the likely effect of the Act. Commentaries upon the success or otherwise of contractual adjudication procedures to date are largely anecdotal and arise in contexts so wholly different[3] from the context in which many adjudications pursuant to the Act will be conducted as to render them worthless as comparators.

The objectives of the Act are laudable,[4] if not entirely necessary.[5] Whether the swift and necessarily approximate procedure of adjudication will be acceptable to the industry will depend upon the industry's willingness to be bound, even on an interim basis, by decisions made in circumstances made necessary by the restrictive timetable laid down by the Act. These circumstances will often include a limited review by the adjudicator of relevant factual material and an incomplete understanding of the applicable law. Many complex construction disputes cannot be properly understood without the expenditure of a great deal of time and therefore money. If the construction industry is content with a less thorough investigation of the facts of a dispute, and the law governing it and equally with the greater risk of misunderstanding and mistake on the part of the decision maker, the adjudication provisions of the Act may achieve acceptance in the industry. If the parties are not satisfied with this sort of rough justice, even on a temporary basis, adjudication under the Act will not satisfy their needs.[6]

Adjudication under the Act provides a new layer of dispute resolution which previously did not exist. It is additional to, and not in substitution for, arbitration or litigation. Whether the right to adjudicate achieves its objectives or increases the expenditure of the industry on dispute resolution will depend upon a complex interrelation of factors including whether the right to adjudication encourages more disputes to be advanced, whether they are subsequently referred for final decision in arbitration or litigation, the ease with which an adjudicator's award may be enforced and the circumstances in which it may be challenged in court. Making the advancement of disputes easier and cheaper will not necessarily make their final resolution easier and cheaper.

---

1 Executive Summary, point 26.
2 Para 9.14.
3 All such adjudications are voluntary in a way that adjudication under the Act is not. They are often conducted to resolve significant disputes on major infrastructure projects within timetables set specifically to accommodate the nature of the dispute which has arisen or is likely to arise.
4 It is assumed that the desire to assist the flow of cash is intended to operate only where cash flow is improperly held up and is not intended to be an objective in its own right.
5 For example, there is no evidence that unresolved disputes resulted in work being held up on site.
6 The desire expressed on a number of occasions during the Hansard debates that the construction industry should be spared the fees of lawyers, can be achieved only if the parties involved in the construction process are willing to forgo their lawyer's services. Time will tell whether adjudication encourages them to do so.

---

## 1.3 What is adjudication?

### 1.3.1 Adjudication, arbitration or expert determination?

It is important to know whether adjudication is the same procedure as arbitration or expert determination. Arbitration and expert determination are each procedures governed by a body of law more or less developed;[7] adjudication is not. If the procedure referred to as 'adjudication' in any particular case is the same procedure as either arbitration or expert determination, it will be governed by the same body of law. If it is not, it will be governed by a law which is under developed, sparse and capable of ascertainment only by a process of reasoning from the general law and, in appropriate cases, by analogy with the law governing arbitration and expert determination.

It will often not be easy to analyse a procedure as arbitration, expert determination or adjudication. This is because these are all procedures with no defined parameters which may blend one into another according to the incidents and effects attached to them by the parties in their contracts. There has been extensive litigation over the boundaries between arbitration and expert determination. This litigation has been conducted largely on the assumption that the categorisation of contractually binding dispute resolution procedures is twofold; namely, arbitration and expert determination. It may be that in years to come a third category called adjudication develops either as an entirely distinct procedure or as a subspecies of expert determination.

None of the Arbitration Acts have defined arbitration and the authoritative text on the subject of arbitration, Mustill and Boyd, *Commercial Arbitration*, 2nd edn (Butterworth 1989) is unable to do so.[8] The Act does not define adjudication but it clearly considers adjudication to be a different procedure from arbitration.[9] Some believe that adjudication is arbitration or alternatively is expert determination. Some procedures which go by the name of adjudication may in fact be arbitration or expert determination. It is beyond the scope of this book to analyse the juridical bases of arbitration, expert determination and adjudication. However, notwithstanding the fluidity of the boundaries between and the similarities of these procedures and the consequent confusion in terminology, it is suggested that they are different, certainly in so far as adjudication is defined in the Act, and they are governed by different legal principles.

## 1.3.2    Adjudication

The *Oxford English Dictionary* describes 'adjudicate' as 'award judicially' and 'try and determine judicially (a claim, etc)', 'pronounce (a person to be)', 'act as a judge in a court, a tribunal, a competition etc'. The judicial dictionaries range in their treatment of adjudication from according no entry for it at all[10] to explaining it expansively as including 'adjudge, arbitrate, award … conclude, decide, decree … determine, determine finally, exercise judicial authority … mediate, order …'.[11] Adjudication has been described by the courts as 'a useful frill' (*Finn Construction Ltd v Lakers Mechanical Services Ltd* (1981) unreported, 12 March) and as of 'an ephemeral and subordinate character which … makes it impossible for a decision to be described as an award on an arbitration agreement' (*A Cameron Ltd v John Mowlem and Co plc* (1995) 52 BLR 24).

Adjudication under the Act requires a decision on a dispute.[12] It is not a procedure such as mediation or conciliation intended to facilitate compromise. It will ordinarily result in a decision of temporary binding effect capable of being overturned in either court or arbitration proceedings.[13] A procedure with interim effect only is neither expert determination nor arbitration. In *A Cameron Ltd v John Mowlem and Co plc* (1995) 52 BLR 24[14] the court considered that because the adjudication clause provided that the adjudicator's decision was 'binding … until' determination by an arbitrator, the adjudication procedure was of 'too ephemeral and subordinate a character' to be described as an arbitration.[15] However, a procedure by which a final and binding decision is to be made (including a procedure which goes by the name of adjudication) may well be an arbitration subject to the full panoply of arbitration laws.[16] Equally, it may be expert determination.

This book is not concerned with arbitration or expert determination. It is concerned only with adjudication. There is no statute or other law which defines adjudication or prescribes the consequences of or the procedure to be followed in an adjudication. For the purposes of compliance with the Act, it does not matter what adjudication is. It matters only that construction contracts make provision complying with s 108. The law concerning adjudication is sparse and the Act does little to change this. The closest analogies to adjudication are arbitration and expert determination. Reasoning by analogy from these procedures is therefore inevitable. Neither analogy is completely appropriate. Notwithstanding, where appropriate, authorities from these areas of law will be cited to indicate how it is believed a court will deal in the context of adjudication with a problem that has arisen in another procedure which is similar, but not the same.

### 1.3.3 Contractual provision to distinguish adjudication

An agreement to refer a dispute to 'adjudication' will not be held automatically and without further analysis not to be an arbitration agreement (*Cape Durasteel Ltd v Rosser & Russell Building Services Ltd* 46 Con LR 75). Whether a particular procedure is an arbitration, an adjudication or an expert determination is a matter of substance and not mere form. Therefore, in any particular case it will be important to ascertain whether a particular procedure has characteristics which require it to be analysed as an arbitration adjudication or expert determination. The name applied by the parties to their chosen procedure is not entirely irrelevant—adjudication, arbitration and expert determination are consensual procedures and if the parties by their contract did not intend arbitration or expert determination and their consequences, but some other procedure, there is a strong argument that the law should not visit upon them the consequences of a consensual procedure to which they did not consent (*Palacath Ltd v Flanagan* [1985] 2 All ER 161). The name chosen for the procedure may be a useful guide to determining the parties' intentions.

It is suggested that the following may assist in characterising a procedure as an adjudication and not an arbitration or expert determination:

(1) The contract should state that the award of the adjudicator is to be of interim effect, binding only until the dispute is finally resolved by some other procedure.

(2) The agreement should state that the procedure is adjudication followed pursuant to s 108 of the Housing Grants, Construction and Regeneration Act 1996.

(3) The agreement should state that the procedure is not an arbitration or expert determination.

(4) The agreement should make express provision to reflect the intention of the parties such that the consequences and effects of the procedure depend upon the agreement of the parties and not upon the legal label attached to the procedure. In doing so, the parties should ensure that the contract complies with s 108 of the Act.

### 1.3.4 Freedom to agree adjudication terms

The Act leaves the parties freedom to agree, within parameters set by s 108, an adjudication scheme to suit their needs. It is not just detail that is left for agreement. The parties are free to reach agreement upon important issues such as whether the adjudicator can determine substantive rights (eg open up certificates), whether he can impose a 'reasonable' or 'commercial' short term solution upon the parties, or whether he must restrict himself to a decision on the merits of the dispute by applying the law to the facts. The parties have freedom to agree procedure provided that the agreed procedure leaves the adjudicator free to take the initiative in ascertaining fact and law.[17] The provision made in these and other important respects will impact upon the nature of the adjudicator's rights and obligations and the essential nature and characteristics of the proceedings.[18]

---

7 Arbitration, in particular, is subject to an extensive body of law recently codified in the Arbitration Act 1996 which regulates important matters such as appeal rights.
8 See p 39.
9 See s 108(3) and (6).
10 *Strouds Judicial Dictionary.*
11 *Burton's Legal Thesaurus.*
12 Section 108(2)(*c*).
13 Section 108(3).
14 Cited with acceptance in *Cape Durasteel Ltd v Rosser & Russell Building Services Ltd* 46 Con LR 75.
15 See, however, Lord Simon in *Arenson v Casson Beckman* [1975] 3 WLR 815 at 824. The statement there that finality and conclusiveness are not necessarily characteristics of arbitration was intended to preclude procedures being deemed quasi arbitral for the purposes of justifying immunity from suit for the decision maker. It did not suggest that a procedure of interim and temporary effect only which was subject to complete rehearing could be arbitration.
16 See *Cape Durasteel Ltd v Rosser and Russell Building Services Ltd* 46 Con LR 75 at page 86 where His Honour Judge Humphrey Lloyd QC stated 'I am unable to accept the submission that "adjudication" is a procedure which cannot be arbitration or that it has an established meaning in construction contracts which precludes it being an arbitration'.
17 Section 108(2)(*f*).
18 The provision made relating to procedure will determine whether the process is a judicial one. This in turn determines matters such as the appropriate rules of evidence to apply and whether the adjudicator is immune from suit under the common law. See paras **4.5.4**; **5.3.4**.

---

## 1.4 Interpreting the Act

The Act was drafted in response to the Latham Report. That report studied the construction industry but not the law governing it. The Act was passed without full consideration of how existing laws would impact upon the new right to adjudication. In these circumstances, it is not possible to say with certainty either precisely what the Act means or how it will be construed. The analysis of the Act in this book is based upon a combination of the following assumptions:

(1) The courts will wish to give effect to the Act as intended by the legislature. A purposive approach to construing the Act—within parameters set by the law—is likely to be adopted.

(2) The courts will not wish to see flagrant or irreparable injustice done in the name of adjudication.

(3) The courts will not wish, in the absence of express power in the contract to the contrary, to allow the adjudication procedure to alter the parties' substantive rights under the contract. It is a procedure intended to ascertain those rights, not change them.

In the context of an area of law introduced by statute which takes the unusual step of prescribing the terms of contracts, which introduces procedures novel to English law and which was passed with some haste, it cannot be said with certainty how the Act will be construed or how the law of adjudication will develop. The most that can be done at this stage is to reason from first principle and by analogy with other contractual dispute resolution techniques, the most appropriate of which are arbitration and expert determination. Analogies from these fields have been relied upon where appropriate. How the courts will reconcile the applicable principles for interpreting the Act will be seen in the years to come. The text in this book is intended as a guide to the likely interpretation

# 2

# The Applicability of the Act

## 2.1 Introduction

As the name suggests, Pt II of the Housing Grants, Construction and Regeneration Act 1996, is intended to apply only to the construction industry. It is inevitable that industry specific legislation will give rise to difficulties of definition—the Act is no different in this respect from any other piece of industry specific legislation. No clear line can be drawn around all activities which are within the construction industry such as to exclude all those which are not.

The right to adjudication created by s 108 of the Act applies only to disputes arising under 'construction contracts'. The term 'construction contract' is defined in s 104 of the Act. This definition relies heavily upon the meaning of 'construction operations' defined in s 105. Section 106 defines construction contracts excluded from the Act (contracts with residential occupiers) and s 107 renders the Act applicable only to contracts in writing (as defined). Section 117 applies the Act to contracts entered into by or on behalf of the Crown (otherwise than by or on behalf of Her Majesty in her private capacity) and to contracts entered into by or on behalf of the Duchy of Cornwall. The Construction Contracts (England and Wales) Exclusion Order 1998 ('The Exclusion Order') excludes further categories of construction contract from the scope of the Act. This chapter deals with the question: when does the Act apply?

## 2.2 Contracts within the Act

### 2.2.1 Territorial application of the Act

By s 104(6)(b), the Act applies only to construction contracts which relate to the carrying out of construction operations in England, Wales or Scotland. It does not apply to Northern Ireland, nor is there any power reserved to the Secretary of State to extend it there. However, it is common for Northern Ireland to institute by Order legislative provisions in similar, if not identical terms to those contained within statutes applying in England and Wales. It is anticipated that Northern Ireland will introduce an Order in substantially similar terms to the Act. The Act applies to all construction contracts within the territorial jurisdiction of England, Wales and Scotland. So, if work is done offshore, for example, on a fixed platform, it may be within the scope of the Act depending on the jurisdiction of the location of the platform.[1]

The Act was designed to create rights and provide statutory protection for the UK construction industry. If construction operations are to be performed in England, Wales or Scotland it is likely, even allowing for the increased market share won by European contractors, that they will be performed by the UK construction industry regardless of the proper law of the contract. Section 104(7) provides that the Act applies if the location of the construction operations is in England, Wales or Scotland whether or not the law of England and Wales or Scotland is the applicable law of the contract. A contract for construction operations abroad, which provides for English law as the proper law of the contract is probably not subject to the Act which in terms applies only if the construction operations are in England, Wales or Scotland. However, the Act applies equally to foreign companies and individuals involved in construction operations in England, Wales or Scotland.

### 2.2.2  Date of contracts covered

By s 104(6)(*a*) the Act applies only to contracts which are entered into after the commencement of Pt II of the Act. Part II of the Act came into force on 1 May 1998. Whether the Act applies must be considered in relation to each contract alone and in isolation from other related contracts in the same suite of contracts or on the same project. So, a main contract entered into before 1 May 1998 will not be subject to the Act while sub-contracts on the same project entered into after 1 May 1998 will be subject to the Act. Equally, a consultant's engagement concluded before 1 May 1998 will not be subject to the Act but if transferred by novation, for example, under a design and build arrangement after 1 May 1998, the novation, being a new contract, is subject to the Act. The parties will need to renegotiate their terms to include provision compliant with the Act or the Scheme will apply.

### 2.2.3  Applicability of the Act to part of the contract

Where a contract relates in part to construction operations which are covered by the Act and in part to other matters which are not, the Act applies pursuant to s 104(5) only in so far as the contract relates to construction operations. For example, a contract in a BOT[2] scheme may include some aspects relating to construction operations and some relating to other matters. A turnkey contract for the construction of a power station will contain some elements which are construction operations and some which are excluded, for example, by s 105(2)(*c*). The parties may provide, but are not obliged to provide by their contract that any dispute arising under the contract, whether it relates to construction operations or not, shall be subject to the adjudication provisions. If it is intended to exclude from the scope of the adjudication provisions those parts of the contract which do not relate to construction operations, this should be done expressly. An adjudication provision without such exclusion may be construed to apply to the entire contract.[3] Any exclusion should be drafted in terms as closely as possible reflecting those appearing in the Act to minimise the risk of inadvertently excluding some activities which are in fact construction operations within the Act, thereby rendering the whole contract non-compliant with s 108.

It is only pursuant to s 104(5) that the Act applies to part only of the contract. Section 104(5) is concerned with circumstances where the contract relates in part to construction operations within s 105 and in part to other matters. There is no provision for the *pro tanto* application of the Act in other circumstances. So, where a contract which relates entirely to construction operations falls in part within and in part outside s 104(1) and (2) the Act applies to the whole contract.

### 2.2.4   Exhaustive definition of construction contract

The Act applies only to construction contracts. The definition of construction contracts in s 104 is exhaustive. The mandatory provisions of the Act do not apply to any agreement which might, in common parlance, ordinary English or common sense properly be said to be a construction contract if it is not within the definition of 'construction contract' within s 104. If the contract is a construction contract within the meaning of the Act, it is not taken outside the Act merely because it is a part of a larger project such as a BOT scheme.

---

1   See Oil & Gas (Enterprise) Act 1982, s 23 and Civil Jurisdiction (Offshore Activities) Order 1987 (SI No 2197).
2   Build, Operate, Transfer.
3   If a contract to which the Act applies in part gives rise to disputes some of which are within and some outside the scope of the Act and the adjudication provisions of the contract, problems may arise over the jurisdiction of the adjudicator to hear claims and cross-claims. See Chapter 7.

---

## 2.3   Construction contract

Section 104(1) defines a 'construction contract' as an agreement for any of the following:
(a)   the carrying out of construction operations;
(b)   the arranging for the carrying out of construction operations by others, whether under sub-contract or otherwise; and
(c)   providing labour for the carrying out of construction operations, whether that labour be the labour of the contracting party or some other person.
A construction contract includes, by s 104(2), an agreement to:
(a)   do architectural, design or surveying work, or
(b)   provide advice on building, engineering, interior or exterior decoration or on the laying out of landscape,
in relation to construction operations.

What constitutes construction operations is a fundamental issue in the assessment of the applicability of the Act. However, it is not all contracts relating to construction operations that are subject to the Act. Rather, it is only those contracts which require the performance of works or rendering of services defined by s 104 in relation to construction operations which fall within the ambit of the Act. So, construction insurance and construction bonds are not generally within the scope of the Act. Construction finance contracts may be within the Act if they provide an obligation upon the borrower to carry out and complete the works in respect of which the finance is provided even though the borrower, usually a developer or employer, is not himself to execute the works but is to procure them from a contractor. However, construction contracts will usually be excluded from the Act.[4] Collateral warranties may or may not be subject to the Act.[5]

### 2.3.1  Carrying out construction operations

Section 104(1)(*a*) is addressed to the physical aspect of carrying out work. So, contracts for the 'carrying out' of construction operations will include main contracts and all levels of sub-contracts to carry out construction operations. Development agreements, party wall agreements, agreements pursuant to s 106 of the Town and Country Planning Act 1990 and s 278 of the Highways Act 1980 and other such contracts undertaking that work will be done will be construction contracts but may be excluded from the scope of the Act by s 3 of the Exclusion Order. In each case, the contract must be scrutinised to ascertain whether one party is undertaking to carry out construction operations and if so, whether the contract is an excluded one.

### 2.3.2  Collateral warranties

Whether collateral warranties are construction contracts within the meaning of the Act depends upon their terms. A collateral warranty which is collateral to another contract, traditionally a main or sub-contract or a professional's terms of appointment may be little more than a simple warranty of quality for work done or to be done. In this case, it will not be a contract for 'the carrying out' of construction operations or any other contract within s 104. However, it is common to see warranties by which the warrantor undertakes 'to carry out and complete work defined in the principal building contract/sub-contract/terms of professional's engagement. This will be a contract for 'the carrying out' or the provision of defined services in relation to construction operations as it undertakes that they will be performed. It is subject to the Act. In each case, the terms of the warranty must be scrutinised in order to assess whether the Act applies.

### 2.3.3  Bonds and guarantees

An undertaking to pay money to compensate the breach of a construction contract committed by another will not be a construction contract within s 104. This is because there is no contract for 'the carrying out' of construction operations or any other contract within s 104. However, a guarantor's obligation might be to guarantee that the debtor performs, to perform itself if the debtor fails, or to pay damages in default of the debtor's or his own performance. Even if, upon proper construction of the guarantee the guarantor's obligation is to perform itself upon failure of the debtor, the contract may fall outside the scope of the Act. Any contract under which the principal obligations include an undertaking by a person to be responsible as surety for the debt or default of another person, including fidelity, advance payment, retention or performance bond is excluded from the Act by s 5(2)(e) of the Exclusion Order.

### 2.3.4  Insurance

Construction insurance contracts will not usually be construction contracts within the meaning of s 104. In any event, contracts of insurance are excluded by s 5(2)(a) of the Exclusion Order. It is necessary here to draw attention to the fact that if an insured liability arises upon the issue of an adjudicator's award, the parties will wish to ensure that their rights against insurers crystallise at that point such that they are not left with an obligation to pay under the award which is not immediately subject to indemnity from insurers. The terms of insurance contracts must be reviewed accordingly. For similar reasons, parties should scrutinise the terms of bonds to ascertain whether the bondsman's liability arises upon the issue of a favourable award or only at some later time.[6]

### 2.3.5  Arranging for the carrying out of construction operations

Section 104(1)(b) is addressed to the procuring of construction operations and includes arranging for the carrying out of construction operations by others whether under sub-contract to him or otherwise. So, for example, management contract, project management or construction management arrangements will fall within s104(1)(b).

### 2.3.6  Provision of labour

Section 104(1)(c) renders the Act applicable to the provision of labour. This sub-section applies the Act to labour only contracts with individuals and contracts for the provision of labour by others. The protections afforded by the Act are offered to individuals employed on a labour only basis, who are often unlikely to be in a position to take full advantage of this part of the Act. They are likely to be engaged under short-term contracts which might not be renewed if they prove too demanding in the exercise of their rights under the Act. Many labour only 'sub-contracts' may upon proper analysis be contracts of employment which are not subject to the Act.

### 2.3.7  Professional services

Section 104(2) includes within the definition of a construction contract various professional services usually employed in the construction industry. Architectural, design and surveying work (which will include certification) in relation to construction operations is covered by s 104(2)(a). Advice is included within s 104(2)(b) However, the professional services habitually provided in relation to construction operations are not completely covered by the express definition of construction contract within s 104(2).

### 2.3.8 Professional services—uncertain cases

Supervision and general contract administration are not expressly covered by the definition of construction contract in s 104(2). Although they may be impliedly covered by the inclusion within s 104(2)(*a*) of 'architectural work', it is not clear what 'architectural work' means. The BSI publication *Glossary of Building and Civil Engineering Terms* defines an architect as 'a person who designs buildings and superintends the execution of building works'. In *R v The Architects Registration Tribunal, ex p Jagger* [1945] 2 All ER 131 it was said that an architect:

'is one who possesses, with due regard to aesthetic as well as practical considerations, adequate skill and knowledge to enable him to (i) originate (ii) design and plan (iii) arrange for and supervise the erection of such building or other works.'

It appears that contract administration as well as design are regarded as primary functions of an architect. As such, they are likely to fall within the scope of 'architectural work' in s 104(2)(*a*).

It is suggested that for the purposes of the Act, 'architectural work' is not limited to work carried out by architects but includes work of a nature traditionally carried out by architects even if in fact carried out by a non-architect. If this is correct, site supervision by an engineer will be within the definition of 'architectural work'. There may be contracts entered into with professionals involved in the construction industry which involve no element of design, advice or surveying work and which are not entered into with architects. Unless the contract administration aspects of a contract are 'architectural work' they will not be included within the Act. There is no reason to believe that the Act intended to exclude such professionals from its scope.

A contract which falls partly within and partly outside s 104 is governed in its entirety by the Act.[8] For this reason it will often not matter precisely what is included within s 104 as most professional contracts will include obligations for design, advice or surveying work. If so, the Act will be applicable also to those parts of the contract which do not fall within the definition in s 104.

### 2.3.9 Contracts of employment

Contracts of employment within the meaning of the Employment Rights Act 1996 are not construction contracts for the purposes of the Act (s 104(3)). This is so even if the employment contract is solely for the carrying out, arranging for the carrying out, provision of labour or professional services in relation to construction operations.

### 2.3.10 Financial services

Construction financing contracts may fall within the scope of the Act if, as is often the case, they contain obligations to build. However they are expressly excluded from the scope of the Act by s 5(2)(*d*) of the Exclusion Order.

### 2.3.11  Power to amend

Section 104(4) gives the Secretary of State power by order to add to, amend or repeal any of the provisions of s 104(1)–(3). Any such order must be laid before and approved by a resolution of each of the Houses of Parliament.

---

4   See also para **2.8.3**.
5   See para **2.3.3**.
6   The ABI model form of guarantee bond is payable, by cl 1, if the damages sustained are 'ascertained pursuant to and in accordance with the provisions of or by reference to the contract and taking into account all sums due or to become due to the Contractor'. This leaves the bondsman with a set-off against the bond money which is outside the adjudication provisions of the contract. A restriction upon set-off against an adjudicator's award in the construction contract may not be effective against a bondsman on the terms of this bond.
7   See, eg *Project Management Agreement and Conditions of Engagement* issued by RICS May 1992.
8   Section 104(5) does not apply to this situation. See para **2.2.3**.

---

## 2.4     Construction operations

'Construction operations' is defined in s 105(1) of the Act, subject to the exclusions contained within s 105(2).[9] The definition contained within s 105(1) is an exhaustive definition and not a definition by generic description. Therefore, if an operation falls within s 105(1) it is a construction operation unless it falls within s 105(2). If it does not fall within s 105(1) it is not a construction operation for the purposes of the Act.

### 2.4.1   Section 105(1)(*a*)

Section 105(1)(*a*) includes:

> 'construction, alteration, repair, maintenance, extension, demolition or dismantling of buildings, or structures forming, or to form, part of the land (whether permanent or not)'.

This part of the definition includes most of the activities traditionally regarded as construction activities including building, refurbishing and demolishing buildings. It was intended that the Act should apply to all trades involved in the construction process, such as plumbers, electricians, joiners and carpenters. Their works can probably be described as the 'construction' of a building or structure or one of the other activities listed in s 105(1)(*a*). It is likely that the applicability of the Act to any particular activity will be construed in the light of the aim of the overall project so that a joinery contract on a project for the construction of a building or structure will be construed as part of the construction process for the purposes of s 105(1)(*a*). Alternatively, such contract would almost certainly fall within the meaning of s 105(1)(*e*) discussed *below*.

It is probably safe to assume that all buildings are structures but that not all structures are buildings (*Mills & Rockleys Ltd v Leicester City Council* [1946] 1 All ER 424). It is likely that 'structure' will be construed 'as coloured by its association

with building' (*Coburg Hotel v London City Council* (1899) 81 LT 450) so as to exclude structures such as cranes and caravans (*British Transport Docks Board v
Williams* [1970] 1 WLR 652 and *R v Welwyn Hatfield District Council, ex p Brinkley*
[1983] JPL 378). Structures may include roads and walls.[10] It is likely that it will
also include tunnels and underground buildings and structures. Section 105(1)(*a*)
is applicable to contracts for the stated activities in relation to both buildings and
structures. Section 105(1)(*a*) includes temporary works which are to form part of
the land.

### 2.4.2   Section 105(1)(*b*)

Section 105(1)(*b*) includes:

> 'construction, alteration, repair, maintenance, extension, demolition or disman-
> tling of any works forming, or to form, part of the land, including (without
> prejudice to the foregoing) walls, roadworks, power-lines, telecommunication
> apparatus, aircraft runways, docks and harbours, railways, inland waterways,
> pipelines, reservoirs, water-mains, wells, sewers, industrial plant and instal-
> lations for purposes of land drainage, coast protection or defence.'

Section 105(1)(*b*) differs from s 105(1)(*a*) in that it includes the stated activities in
relation to any 'works' as opposed to 'buildings' or 'structures' forming, or to
form, part of the land. Temporary works are not included but if the 'works' within
s 105(1)(*b*) are also 'buildings' or 'structures' within s 105(1)(*a*) temporary works
will be within the scope of the Act by virtue of the latter section if not by virtue of
the former. Most of the activities listed can be described as works of civil engineering. 'Works' within s 105(1)(*b*) should not be so restricted as the works specifically listed are expressly said to be without prejudice to the generality of the
opening words of the section.

### 2.4.3   Section 105(1)(*c*)

Section 105(1)(*c*) includes:

> 'installation in any building or structure of fittings forming part of the land,
> including (without prejudice to the foregoing) systems of heating, lighting, air
> conditioning, ventilation, power supply, drainage, sanitation, water supply or
> fire protection, or security or communications systems.'

The detailed fittings specifically listed can all be classified as works of plumbing
or mechanical or electrical engineering. They are stated, however, to be without
prejudice to the opening words of s 105(1)(*c*), namely, the 'installation … of fittings forming part of the land'. Therefore, the installation of fittings forming part
of the land, such as fitted furniture, tiling, fitted bedrooms, bathrooms and kitch-
ens, even possibly carpet laying will be covered by the definition of construction
operations within s 105(1)(*c*). Many of these activities may not really be activities
within the construction industry to which the Act was intended to apply.
     'Fitting' has been considered in the context of the law governing freehold and

leasehold property. It is common for conveyances to include covenants relating to fittings and fixtures. The authority originating from this area of the law may be helpful in the construction of s 108(1)(*c*) but is unlikely to be definitive of the meaning of 'fitting' within the Act. Covenants in conveyances are intended for a purpose unrelated to the construction industry.

### 2.4.4   Section 105(1)(*d*)

Section 105(1)(*d*) includes:

> 'external or internal cleaning of buildings and structures, so far as carried out in the course of their construction, alteration, repair, extension or restoration.'

Cleaning as an integral part of construction works is included within the Act. Cleaning as part of the routine maintenance and operation of buildings is not. This section is not expressly limited to buildings and structures which form or are to form part of the land but it is suggested that it will be construed as so limited. The extent to which this section might otherwise apply is endless.[11]

### 2.4.5   Section 105(1)(*e*)

Section 105(1)(*e*) includes:

> 'operations which form an integral part of, or are preparatory to, or are for rendering complete, such operations as are previously described in this subsection, including site clearance, earth moving, excavation, tunnelling and boring, laying of foundations, erection, maintenance or dismantling of scaffolding, site restoration, landscaping and the provision of roadways and other access works.'

All activities and the works of each and every trade could not be specifically defined in the Act. Therefore, s 105(1)(*e*) contains a 'mop up' provision.

The detailed list of operations at the end of s 105(1)(*e*) is prefaced by the word 'including' but not 'without prejudice to the foregoing' which appears in s 105(1)(*b*) and (*c*). It is unlikely that the draftsman intended to exclude the *ejusdem generis* rule in respect of ss 105(1)(*b*) and (*c*) but not in respect of s105(1)(*e*). Given the generality of the opening words of s 105(1)(*e*) and the intention to include within the definition of construction operations all activities integral to the main activities listed in the other subsections of s 105(1), the omission of the words 'without prejudice to the foregoing' is more likely to be a recognition that the matters listed are of so diverse a nature as to leave little scope for the *ejusdem generis* rule.

Operations integral or preparatory to the operations previously described will include such matters as setting out, obtaining statutory consents, drawing office work, crane hire, site clearance and multi service gang work etc. There will be some activities whose status under s 105(1)(*e*) is unclear. For example, site security is often provided in relation to construction operations but it may be said not to form an integral part of, be preparatory to or be for rendering complete the activities specifically listed in s 105(1)(*a*)–(*c*).

### 2.4.6   Section 105(1)(f)

Section 105(1)(f) includes 'painting or decorating the internal or external surfaces of any building or structure'.

There may be a semantic difference between 'painting' with paint and the application of substances in liquid form, such as creosote. However, it is unlikely that a court will be attracted by a narrow construction of the Act. 'Painting' is therefore likely to be held to include the application of liquid substances such as creosote and sealants. The application of non-liquid substances such as renders will usually be included within one of the other subsections of s 105.[12] 'Buildings' and 'structures' under this section are probably limited to those forming or to form part of the land.[13]

### 2.4.7   Works

If those activities specifically listed as 'works' in s 105(1)(b) are not also 'buildings' or 'structures' within s 105(1)(a), (c)–(f), those parts of a contract for the installation of fittings or the cleaning or painting of 'works' will not be within the scope of the Act. So, the painting of road markings, markings on aircraft runways, docks and harbours, etc will be excluded from the Act. It is suggested, however, that most if not all of the 'works' listed in s 105(1)(b) are also 'structures' within s 105(1)(a),(c)–(f).

### 2.4.8   Forming or to form part of the land

Section 105(1)(a)–(c) expressly and s 105(1)(d) and (f) impliedly restrict the definition of construction operations to buildings, structures or works forming or to form part of the land[14]. The authorities dealing with what forms part of the land arise most commonly in the context of leasehold property. Care should be taken when transposing these authorities directly into the different context of s 105. The principles which have developed in the context of leasehold property may, however, be useful with appropriate adaptation in the context of the Act. As a general rule, although not without exception, if a structure is not affixed to the ground but rests on the ground by virtue of its own weight alone it does not form part of the land (*Pole-Carew v Western Counties & General Manure Co* [1920] 2 Ch 97). If it can be severed from the ground without significant damage and still be capable of viable use it does not form part of the land. If it was affixed to the land for temporary purposes and not for the permanent improvement or change in the land but for the more complete enjoyment of it as a chattel it will not form part of the land.

In the recent House of Lords decision of *Elitestone Ltd v Morris* (1997) unreported, 1 May, the issue of whether a structure (in this case a bungalow) formed part of the land for the purposes of protection under the Rent Act 1977 was held to depend, not upon whether it was affixed to the ground or rested upon its own weight, but upon the question whether it could be taken down and re-erected elsewhere without being destroyed in the process. If it could not, there was a strong inference that it was intended to and had become part of the realty. Lord

Browne Wilkinson regarded the issue, to a certain extent, as one of common sense and considered that while the degree of annexation may be a useful test when considering such items as tapestries etc it was less useful when considering large items such as houses. A distinction was drawn between such a structure as was considered in this case and a Portakabin or mobile home and the fact that such buildings may be attached to the land for the purposes of obtaining mains services such as water or electricity was not thought to be relevant. So, the construction of portable buildings and other moveable structures, such as Dutch barns, moveable shelters, exhibition homes, tents and marquees will not form part of the land. Mobile homes may or may not form part of the land depending upon the permanence of their fixture to the land.

### 2.4.9   What is land?

In most cases the question of what is land will not give rise to difficulty. Land includes land covered by water,[15] such as riverbeds, causeways, ponds and lakes. It also includes the sea bed within the territorial jurisdiction of the Act.[16] The erection of buildings, structures or works[17] on the sea bed may therefore be construction operations within the Act. The construction of fixed[18] oil or other platforms and associated plant on the sea bed will usually be excluded by section 105(2)(c). The construction of facilities such as accommodation on the platform will not be excluded.

---

9   The definition is taken from the Income and Corporation Taxes Act 1988.
10   These will also be 'works' within s 105(1)(b).
11   The following may be structures which do not form part of the land: exhibits at 'Ideal Homes' exhibitions, caravans, cranes, aeroplanes, space stations etc.
12   Eg s 105(1)(e).
13   See para **2.4.4**.
14   See para **2.4.4**.
15   Interpretation Act 1978, Sched 1. See also the interesting case of *Thames Heliport plc v Tower Hamlets London Borough Council* (1996) *The Times*, 10 December.
16   See para **2.2.1**.
17   Such as in connection with the underwater laying of pipelines or oil platforms.
18   Floating platforms may be outside the Act as not forming part of the land. This will depend upon the manner and permanence of their attachment to sea bed installations.

---

## 2.5   What is excluded?

### 2.5.1   Section 105(2)

Section 105(2) sets out a list of activities which are not construction operations. The definition of what is a construction operation within s 105(1) is exhaustive. There should, therefore, be no need to exclude any activity unless that activity would, but for the exclusion, have been included within s 105(1).

### 2.5.2   Section 105(2)(a)

Section 105(2)(a) excludes: 'drilling for, or extraction of, oil or natural gas'. This exclusion applies to onshore and offshore drilling or extraction of oil or natural gas. This activity is not part of the construction industry and is not perceived to be subject to the same problems as encountered in the construction industry such as to justify the applicability of the Act. However, the construction of buildings or structures for use in connection with the drilling or extraction of oil or natural gas will be within s 105(1) and is not excluded by s 105(2)(*a*). It is not easy to see how 'drilling' or 'extraction' of oil or natural gas could be regarded as included within s 105(1) such as to require exclusion by s 105(2)(*a*).

### 2.5.3    Section 105(2)(*b*)

Section 105(2)(*b*) excludes: 'extraction (whether by underground or surface working) of minerals; tunnelling or boring, or construction of underground works, for this purpose'.

The extraction of minerals does not fall within s 105(1) and does not require the express exclusion contained within s 105(2)(*b*). Tunelling, boring and the construction of underground works for the purposes of the extraction of minerals does require the express exclusion provided by this subsection. Construction of overground works are not excluded.

### 2.5.4    Section 105(2)(*c*)

Section 105(2)(*c*) excludes:

'assembly, installation or demolition of plant or machinery, or erection or demolition of steelwork for the purposes of supporting or providing access to plant or machinery, on a site where the primary activity is—

(i)  nuclear processing, power generation, or water or effluent treatment, or
(ii)  the production, transmission, processing or bulk storage (other than warehousing) of chemicals, pharmaceuticals, oil, gas, steel or food and drink.'

The activities listed above were regarded by the legislature as process engineering activities. Process engineering was explained in Parliament as industrial work involving certain types of chemical, physical or biological processes. Examples were said to include refining oil, generating electricity and making chocolate. The process engineering industry was intended to be excluded from the scope of the Act as it was felt that this industry does not suffer from the litigation and claims oriented attitude from which the building and civil engineering industries suffer.[19]

It will be a question of fact whether in any particular case the primary purpose of a site is nuclear processing, power generation, water or effluent treatment or the production, transmission, processing or bulk storage of chemicals, pharmaceuticals, oil, gas, steel, or food and drink. Although 'food and drink' is expressed in conjunctive terms it will probably be construed in disjunctive terms so that the stated activities in relation to the production, etc of food *or* drink is excluded.

It is not all construction work in relation to the sites listed which is excluded by s 105(2)(c). It is only the assembly, installation or demolition of plant or machinery or erection or demolition of steelwork providing support or access to it on such sites that is excluded. Therefore, constructing the superstructure of the building housing the plant and machinery will be within the Act as will be the work of all other trades not expressly excluded.

A distinction is to be drawn between where the primary purpose of the site is the 'storage' of chemicals, pharmaceuticals, oil, gas, steel or food and drink and where the primary purpose of the site is the 'warehousing' of those products. Where the primary purpose is storage, the assembly, installation or demolition of plant or machinery etc will be excluded from the Act. Where it is warehousing, it will not be excluded. The difference between storage and warehousing is intended to reflect the difference between construction and process engineering. It was said in Parliament that when products are packed or bottled and stored, they are warehoused.[20] So, the listed activities in relation to a storage facility for a supermarket to store packed or bottled products will be within the Act—the construction is not part of a product making facility.

### 2.5.5   Section 105(2)(d)

Section 105(2)(d) excludes:

'manufacture or delivery to site of—
(i)   building or engineering components or equipment;
(ii)  materials, plant or machinery; or
(iii) components for systems of heating, lighting, air conditioning, ventilation, power supply, drainage, sanitation, water supply or fire protection, or for security or communications systems;

except under a contract which also provides for their installation.'

The manufacturing and delivery industries are not within the mischief intended to be corrected by the Act. Nor are they within the definition of 'construction operations', s 105(1). Supply only contracts are excluded by s 105(2)(d). Supply and fit contracts are not excluded. It is not possible, pursuant to s 104(5), to disapply the adjudication provisions to the supply aspects of a supply and fit contract. This is because s 105(2)(d) does not allow the distinction of the supply aspects of a supply and fit contract.

### 2.5.6   Section 105(2)(e)

Section 105(2)(e) excludes 'the making, installation and repair of artistic works, being sculptures, murals and other works which are wholly artistic in nature'.

The making, installation or repair of pieces of artwork which have artistic value but no practical function falls outside the scope of the Act. If part of a building, structure or other works which does have a practical function is clothed in artwork, the Act does apply. In this case, the works are not 'wholly artistic in nature'.

### 2.5.7   Power to amend

By s 105(3) the Secretary of State may by order add to, amend or repeal any of the provisions of s 105(1) or (2) provided that such order shall have been laid before and approved by a resolution of each House of Parliament.

---

19   Viscount Ullswater, 570 HL Official Report, Thursday 28 March 1996 (No 70).
20   Earl Ferrers, 570 HL Official Report, Thursday 28 March 1996 (No 70).

---

## 2.6   Excluded contracts

The only construction contracts excluded from the operation of Pt II of the Act are:
(a)   construction contracts with a residential occupier—s 106(1)(*a*); and
(b)   any other description of construction contract excluded from the operation of the Act by order of the Secretary of State—s 106(1)(*b*).

### 2.6.1   Residential occupier

A contract with a residential occupier is defined by s 106(2) as a construction contract which principally relates to operations on a dwelling which one of the parties to the contract occupies, or intends to occupy, as his residence. It need not be his only or even his main residence so it is probably the case that a holiday home will be a residence. The intention to let the holiday home for profit may render it more likely that it is not intended to be occupied as a residence but ultimately the question will be one of fact and degree. 'Dwelling' means a dwelling house or flat. 'Dwelling house' does not include a building containing a flat and 'flat' means a separate and self-contained premise constructed or adapted for residential use and forming part of a building from some other part of which the premises are divided horizontally.[21] The definition of dwelling house to exclude a building containing a flat prevents a quasi-commercial construction project from being excluded from the Act because one part of the building is to be occupied as his residence by a party to the contract. However, this definition may also prevent a residential occupier of premises with a granny flat from relying on the exclusion in s 106.

It is possible that on the wording of s 106 the residential occupier exclusion cannot apply to new build works for the construction of a dwelling which one party intends to occupy as his residence. This construction may be justified by a narrow interpretation of s 106 to the effect that construction operations cannot be carried out 'on' a dwelling which does not yet exist. The question whether the Act applies to the construction of new dwellings which one party to the contract intends to occupy as his residence does not arise only in the relatively occasional case of an individual commissioning works for the construction of his residence. It arises also in relation to the national housebuilder who sells direct to the public. A contract for the sale or conveyance of a dwelling is not within the scope of the Act. However, a contract for the sale of a dwelling at some time in the future coupled with an obligation to build and/or complete construction works on that dwelling will be a contract for 'the carrying out' of construction operations within s 104(1)(*a*) of the Act.[22] It is likely that a court, taking a purposive approach to the interpretation of the Act will hold the exclusionary provisions of s 106 to cover works for the construction of a new dwelling. To interpret s 106 in any other way would subject such a contract not only to the adjudication provisions of s 108, but also to the obligation to make interim payment for the construction works pursuant to s 109. This could create serious difficulties for the purchasers involved, particularly with respect to their mortgage arrangements. For this reason, a restrictive interpretation of s 106 is unattractive.

### 2.6.2   Power to amend

The terms of s 106(1)(*b*) suggest that the Secretary of State may exclude from the operation of the Act, construction contracts other than those with a residential occupier. This is probably not the case. The power to amend s 106 is conferred on the Secretary of State by s 106(3). This subsection empowers the Secretary of State to amend only subs (2). Subsection (2) does no more than provide a definition of a residential occupier. Therefore, whilst the Secretary of State has power to amend the definition of a residential occupier, he cannot exclude from the operation of the Act other types of construction contracts. Subsection (2) of s 106 may be amended by Order, provided that a draft has been laid before and approved by a resolution of each of the Houses of Parliament as required by s 106(4).

---

21  See s 106(2).
22  Sub-contracts and contracts between builders and their professionals will not be excluded by s 106.

---

## 2.7     Contracts in writing

The provisions of Pt II of the Act are, by s 107(1),[23] applicable only where the contract is in writing. In circumstances where the aim of the Act was to provide certain mandatory protections for those engaged in the construction industry and to simplify dispute resolution procedures, it is not clear why the Act should be made to apply only to contracts in writing. Contracts in writing are widely defined by s 107, but there is little logic in excluding from the Act purely oral contracts or construction operations not carried out under contract. The rationale of the Act applies with no less force than in the case of an agreement in writing. The structure of the Act requiring certain contractual provision to be made is not easily accommodated within purely oral contracts. It is not accommodated at all if there is no contract. However, it is intended that where there is a contract in writing which does not make contractual provision complying with s 108, the Scheme will apply. There is no reason why the Scheme or some variant thereon should not apply equally in the case of oral contracts or construction operations not carried out under contract. If a contract which is not in writing contains adjudication provisions they will be enforced no less than if the contract were in writing but it need not contain adjudication provisions at all or comply with s 108.

In addition to the disapplication of the Act to any contract save one in writing as defined within s 107, this section contains the following mysterious wording: 'and any other agreement between the parties as to any matter is effective for the purposes of this Part only if in writing'.

This wording is obscure but is probably intended to achieve the result that the contractual adjudication provisions must be in writing to be effective[24]. So, a written agreement to terms orally expressed may be a contract in writing within s 107(2) but by reason of s 107(1), the adjudication provisions, to be effective, must also be in writing. If they are not, there may be a written contract but by reason of the fact that the adjudication provisions are not in writing, they will not be effective, the contract will be non-compliant with the Act and the Scheme will apply. This result appears to follow even if the adjudication provision is in writing save for a minor oral variation.

### 2.7.1   Part oral contracts

It is possible to have a contract which is partly in writing and partly oral. The Act gives no guidance as to its applicability in such a case. However, s 107 draws a distinction between an agreement in writing (s 107(2)) and terms in writing (s 107(3)). If the agreement is in writing but the terms are oral in part or in whole, there will be a contract in writing within s 107(2). If the agreement is oral but makes reference to terms which are in writing, the contract is in writing by s 107(3). Where the oral agreement refers to terms in writing but supplements or qualifies them orally, it is not clear that such contract falls within the meaning of s 107(3).

### 2.7.2   Contract in writing

Section 107(2) states that there is an agreement in writing if:
(a)   the agreement is made in writing (whether or not it is signed by the parties);
(b)   the agreement is made by exchange of communications in writing; or
(c)   the agreement is evidenced in writing.
Section 107(3) states that where the parties agree otherwise than in writing by reference to terms which are in writing, they make an agreement in writing.

Section 107(4) provides that an agreement is evidenced in writing if an agreement made otherwise than in writing is recorded by one of the parties, or by a third party, with the authority of the parties to the agreement.

The definitions of contracts in writing contained within s 107(2)(a)–(c) and (3) may overlap. There is no point in attempting to set out exhaustively what sort of agreement will fall within each of the specific provisions defining a contract in writing. Many agreements will fall into more than one category. A standard form signed or otherwise executed by the parties will be an agreement in writing within s 107(2)(a). A standard form not signed but agreed orally will be an agreement in writing pursuant to s 107(3). A contract agreed by exchange of correspondence will be an agreement in writing pursuant to s 107(2)(b) and, possibly, s 107(2)(a). If the parties agree in writing to terms orally expressed, this will be an agreement in writing within s 107(2)(c).

Where the parties agree orally and one records that agreement that may, by virtue of s 107(4) be an agreement in writing within s 107(2)(c). It is not clear if the party recording the agreement needs the authority of the other parties before a contract in writing comes into existence or whether such authority is needed only if it is a third party who records the agreement. The wording of s 107(3) is unclear. It is considered that the latter view is a preferable interpretation as it maximises the scope of the Act, although the punctutation of the subsection appears to support the former view.

### 2.7.3   Legal submissions

Section 107(5) states that an exchange of written submissions in adjudication proceedings or in arbitral or legal proceedings in which the existence of an agreement otherwise than in writing is alleged by one party against another party and not denied by the other party in his response constitutes as between those parties an agreement in writing to the effect alleged. This provision requires an uncontroverted plea of an oral contract to be treated for the purposes of the Act as an agreement in writing 'to the effect alleged'.

The 'effect alleged' can only sensibly relate to the existence of the contract alleged and not to its form or any of its terms. Otherwise, it would be within the power of one party, by alleging an oral contract which is agreed, to fix in its pleading the terms of that contract leaving the other party no right to deny the terms alleged. Section 107 should operate to bring what would otherwise be an oral contract within the scope of the Act. It should not have the wider effect open on the wording of the section of allowing the pleading of an oral contract to determine the terms of that contract.

It will be rare that a claimant in adjudication proceedings alleges a contract otherwise than in writing. If he does so, he is alleging that the adjudicator has no jurisdiction. It is not clear whether the conclusive effect of s 107(5) arises upon the parties' initial pleadings such as effectively to prevent them from amending their pleadings in this regard. If so, the practical consequence may be that contracts pleaded as being otherwise than in writing may be denied as a matter of course in order to avoid conclusiveness under s 107(5).

### 2.7.4   Recording

Section 107(6) provides that reference in Pt II to anything being written or in writing includes reference to it being recorded by any means. This includes recording by means not relying upon the written word on paper or in electronic or code form. Video or tape recordings although rare will amount to writing under the Act.

### 2.7.5   No contract

It is likely that the expansive definition of contract in writing found in s 107 will cover the majority of construction contracts, which are usually either signed, concluded by exchange of correspondence or, if purely oral, at least noted by one of the parties. It will be rare that a completely oral construction contract otherwise within the scope of the Act is entered into.[25] However, the issue of whether terms are incorporated into an agreement remains in the context of adjudication as it does in arbitration (see *Aughton (formerly Aughton Group) v M F Kent Services Ltd* 57 BLR 1 and subsequent cases.)

It will not, however, be rare that an exchange of correspondence, properly analysed, is found not to constitute a contract at all. Letters of intent may or may not evidence contracts. Communications in writing may or may not result in concluded contracts. It is, therefore, unfortunately the case that letters of intent and other correspondence must be analysed for the purposes of ascertaining whether there is any contract at all sufficient to found jurisdiction in the adjudicator to resolve disputes arising under it.

---

23  Taken from s 5 of the Arbitration Act 1996.
24  This wording appears in s 5 of the Arbitration Act 1996. Its logic there of ensuring that the consensual procedure of arbitration applies only to those who can demonstrably (in writing) be shown to have agreed to arbitration applies with less force in the non-consensual context of adjudication.
25  Obligations undertaken by deed which is not also a contract will not fall within the Act.

---

## 2.8   The Exclusion Order

The Exclusion Order was laid before Parliament on 18 December 1997 and re-laid on 12 January 1998. It excludes from the Act certain contracts which are, technically, construction contracts under the Act but to which the Act was not designed to apply. The Exclusion Order 1998 (SI No 648) is exhaustive and does not exclude contracts within broad categories. It excludes contracts satisfying closely defined criteria and if these criteria are not met, there is no room for the argument that a particular contract bears similar characteristics to one excluded if it is not in fact excluded. The four categories of excluded contracts are dealt with below.

### 2.8.1   Agreements under statute

The following statutory agreements are excluded (s 3):
(a)  agreements under ss 38 or 278 of the Highways Act 1980;
(b)  agreements under ss 106, 106A or 299A of the Town and Country Planing Act 1990;
(c)  agreements under s 104 of the Water Industry Act 1991;
(d)  externally financed development agreements under s 1 of the National Health Service (Private Finance) Act 1997.

### 2.8.2   Private Finance Initiative

Section 4 excludes contracts entered into under the Private Finance Initiative (PFI) as defined in the Exclusion Order. PFI is not a term of art and has therefore been closely defined. In order to fall within the definition as set out in the Exclusion

Order, the contract must satisfy each one of a number of conditions. These conditions are:

(1)  The contract must contain a statement that it is entered into under the PFI initiative or under a project applying similar principals.

(2)   The consideration due under the contract must be determined at least in part by reference to a defined standard of post construction performance. These are the standards attained in the performance of a service, the provision of which is the principal purpose(s) for which the building or structure is constructed; the extent, rate or intensity of use of all or any part of the building or structure in question or the right to operate any facility in connection with the building or structure.

(3)   One of the parties to the contract must be:

  (a)  a Minister of the Crown; or

  (b)  a department in respect of which appropriation accounts are required to be prepared under the Exchequer and Audit Departments Act 1866; or

  (c)  any other authority or body whose accounts are required to be examined and certified by or are open to the inspection of the Comptroller and Auditor General by virtue of an agreement entered into before the commencement date or by virtue or any enactment; or

  (d)  any authority or body listed in Sched 4 to the National Audit Act 1983 (nationalised industries and other public authorities); or

  (e)  a body whose accounts are subject to audit by auditors appointed by the Audit Commission; or

  (f)  the governing body or trustees of a voluntary school withing the meaning of s 31 of the Education Act 1994; or

  (g)  a company wholly owned by any of the bodies at (a)–(e) above.

Thus, notwithstanding that a contract may be a construction contract within the definition of the Act, it is excluded if it is a PFI contract, the essence of which is that payment for the construction works is not a discrete obligation payable directly as the works progress but is recouped during the operation of the facility constructed. Construction contracts entered into by a party to a PFI contract (eg contracts with professionals or subcontractors) are not excluded. This is because the contracts will not have one of the persons listed in s 4(c) as one of their party's.

## 2.8.3  Finance agreements

The Exclusion Order recognises that the definition of construction contract under the Act is a broad one and encompassed not only contracts within the construction industry but also contracts within a range of service industries. There is therefore an exemption for many of these contracts. The excluded contracts are (s 5):

(1)  Contracts of insurance. Most standard construction insurance contracts do not fall within the definition of construction contracts under the Act but the Exclusion Order has put the matter beyond doubt. Insurance contracts are excluded from the Act. However construction contracts which contain obligations of an insurance nature are not excluded.[26]

(2)  Any contract under which the principal obligations include the formation or dissolution of a company, unincorporated association or partnership. So, the

formation or dissolution of joint ventures, whatever their legal form, even if they contain construction obligations, are excluded. However, construction contracts entered into by such companies, partnerships or unincorporated associations are not excluded.[27]

(3) Any contract under which the principal obligations include the creation or transfer of securities or any right or interest in securities. Contracts creating charges over property or companies are excluded but construction contracts which create charges (eg over material or equipment on site) will usually not be excluded as the creation of the security will not be the principal obligation under the contract.

(4) Any contract under which the principal obligations include the lending of money. Construction finance contracts are therefore excluded.

(5) Any contract under which the principal obligations include an undertaking by a person to be responsible as surety for the debt or default of another person, including a fidelity bond, advance payment bond, retention or performance bond. It will also include a bid bond.

In any particular case, whether a contract is excluded will depend upon an analysis of the contract concerned. The question whether one of the principal obligations is an excluded one will depend entirely upon the terms of the contract.

### 2.8.4 Development agreements

Development agreements are excluded from the scope of the Act (s 6). Excluded development agreements are defined as agreements which contain provision for the grant or disposal of a relevant interest in land on which takes place the principal construction operations to which the contract relates. Relevant interest in land means a freehold or leasehold interest but to be excluded the leasehold interest must expire no earlier that 12 months after the completion of the construction operations under the contract.

### 2.8.5 Conclusion

There will inevitably be borderline cases in respect of which it may be difficult to tell whether the contract is an excluded one or not. There are also likely to be parties whose commercial interests are best served by alleging or denying that a particular contract is an excluded one. However, in most instances, what constitutes an excluded contract will be plain. The exclusion from the scope of the Act of contracts which the Latham report did not consider and to which the Act was not designed to apply can only be a benefit and play a major role in preventing the Act from falling into disrepute.

---

26  See FIDIC 4th edn, cl 65.3 and 65.5.

---

## 2.9    Jurisdictional consequences

A party intent on derailing the adjudication procedure is given ammunition within s 107 with which to do so. There may be disputes in any particular case giving rise to the following questions: is there a contract at all? If there is a contract, is it a construction contract and is it in writing? If so, is it on terms containing written adjudication provisions? If the answer to any of these questions is no, the Act may not apply at all, or the Scheme may apply. Disputes as to how disputes are to be resolved—in accordance with the Act or not—may prolong the overall time-table of whatever is the appropriate dispute resolution procedure and render the right to a swift adjudication more illusory than real.

# 3

# The Jurisdictional
# Requirements of the Act

## 3.1 Introduction

### 3.1.1 Section 108(1) provides:

> 'A party to a construction contract has the right to refer a dispute arising under the contract for adjudication under a procedure complying with this section.
>
> For this purpose, dispute includes any difference.'

Section 108(1) creates the right to adjudication and defines the circumstances in which it arises. The right is limited to those engaged in construction contracts, but is otherwise of wide effect. Any dispute arising under the contract may be referred to adjudication at any time.

### 3.1.2 No interference with related procedures

Section 108 creates a right to adjudication but does not impose an obligation upon any party to seek the resolution of his dispute in adjudication.[1] It does not seek to remove or replace other rights of dispute resolution, for example, arbitration. Nor does s 108 restrict the implementation of such other rights during an adjudication procedure or *vice versa*. The Act does not require adjudication to be a condition precedent to other means of dispute resolution. The parties are free to seek the resolution of their dispute by adjudication or any other available procedure as and when they see fit.

### 3.1.3 Contractual regulation of related procedures

The parties may by their contract regulate the interrelation of adjudication and other dispute resolution procedures. The contract should not restrict the time when a dispute may be referred to adjudication—that would be inconsistent with s 108(2)(*a*). However, the contract may restrict the time when arbitration and possibly court proceedings[2] may be commenced. For example, the contract may provide that there may be no court or arbitration proceedings until after, say, completion of the works. The contract may also provide for adjudication to be a condition precedent to court or arbitration proceedings. Such a provision will be enforced (*Channel Tunnel Group Ltd v Balfour Beatty Ltd* [1993] 2 WLR 262).

### 3.1.4   Status of the right to adjudication

The right to adjudication under the Act is of statutory origin—it is expressly created by s 108(1). If the contract makes provision for adjudication, the right becomes a contractual one also. Even if the contract does not make provision for adjudication complying with s 108, the right is statutory and contractual, for the Scheme applies and by s 114(4) the Scheme has effect as implied terms of the contract. If the contract contains workable adjudication terms, the right to adjudicate in accordance with these terms is not affected by the Act even if the contractual adjudication terms are non-compliant with s 108 such that the Scheme also applies. This raises the spectre of two adjudications over the same issue, one under the Scheme and one under the contractual adjudication terms, each resulting in different conclusions. A possible argument that the Scheme ousts the express contractual provisions is difficult as implied terms of a contract (s 114(4)) cannot ordinarily oust express terms.

### 3.1.5   Status of adjudicator's award

An adjudicator's decision given under a contract containing adjudication terms whether or not they comply with s 108 is entirely contractual in status. Section 108 creates a right to adjudicate but it is only the contract that creates the obligation to comply with the adjudicator's decision. The Scheme also has contractual status.[3]

### 3.1.6   Jurisdiction

Each of the requirements of s 108(1) defines the adjudicator's jurisdiction. If not satisfied, the adjudicator has no jurisdiction to make an award. There is no however, reason why the adjudicator should not make an initial assessment of his own jurisdiction without prejudice to the parties' rights subsequently to challenge the adjudicator's award on the grounds of lack of jurisdiction. A party who objects to the jurisdiction of the adjudicator should do so expressly at the earliest moment. If he fails expressly to raise any such objection, it may be deemed to have been waived. There is, however, no statutory requirement to this effect and no equivalent in the context of adjudication of s 31 of the Arbitration Act 1996.

The greater the scope for jurisdictional (or any other) challenge to the adjudicator's award, the less effective will be the adjudication procedure for settling disputes on an interim basis. The Act is structured and drafted in such a way that a number of jurisdictional obstacles must be overcome before the right to adjudication arises. This creates scope for parties to raise jurisdictional challenges to the adjudicator's award with a view to resisting enforcement.

---

1   Section 108, on its face, allows one party to refer a claim made by another to adjudication. See Chapter 7.

2   It is arguable that any restriction on the time when court proceedings may be commenced is against public policy as temporarily ousting the jurisdiction of the court. This argument becomes less convincing as the courts become increasingly willing to allow dispute resolution procedures such as arbitration, expert determination and adjudication to oust the jurisdiction of the court permanently.

3   See s 114(4).

## 3.2   Party to a construction contract

### 3.2.1   Parties

The right to adjudication created by s 108 is conferred only upon parties to construction contracts. Rights to adjudication and subsequent rights to enforce an adjudicator's award will not be available to or bind any person not party to the contract, such as a bondsman securing the performance of a contractor. The contractual right to adjudication and the contractual right to enforce an adjudicator's award may be transferred in the same way and subject to the same conditions as any other contractual right.

### 3.2.2   Agents

If the servant or agent of a party to a construction contract is pursued personally for some act or omission during the course of the contract that servant or agent will not be a party to a construction contract for the purposes of s 108. A principal liable for the act or default of an agent may be a party to a construction contract. If an agent is sued as agent for an undisclosed principal, he becomes liable on the contract personally[4] and is a party thereto for the purposes of s 108. An agent sued for breach of warranty of authority is probably sued upon a contract[5] and may in appropriate circumstances be subject to s 108.

### 3.2.3   Employees

A contract of employment under the Employment Rights Act 1996 cannot amount to a construction contract.[6]

### 3.2.4   Assignees and novatees

An assignee of the rights created by a construction contract is not a party to that contract. He may, however, acquire the right to adjudicate pursuant to his assignment. The burden of the contract does not pass on assignment so an assignee cannot be pursued in adjudication.[7] A person who acquires rights and subjects himself to burdens under a construction contract by novation will be subject to s 108. A person such as a funder of the project who exercises step in rights other than under a novation may not be subject to s 108.

### 3.2.5   Liquidators, receivers and administrators

The liquidator of a company which was party to a construction contract will not be party to the construction contract for the purposes of s 108. A receiver is agent for the company until a liquidator is appointed. He is not a party to the contract.

The company may be entitled to claim and be pursued in adjudication notwithstanding the appointment of a liquidator, receiver or administrator. The provisions of ss 10(1)(c), 11(3)(d) and 130(2) of the Insolvency Act 1986, which require leave of the court before 'proceedings' can be commenced or continued against a company in liquidation or administration, may or may not apply to the commencement or continuance of adjudication proceedings. Whether they apply depends upon whether adjudication is held to be a 'proceeding' for the purposes of those statutes.

There may be little practical merit in pursuing in adjudication a company in liquidation, receivership or administration for, in the event of a successful claim, even if enforced by court proceedings (for which leave would be required pursuant to ss 10(1)(c), 11(3)(d) and 130(2) of the Insolvency Act 1986), the claimant may have achieved little more than a ranking as an unsecured creditor. It may well have ranked as such even before the adjudication procedure. A company in liquidation, receivership or administration or otherwise of questionable solvency may derive little benefit from pursuing a claim in adjudication proceedings for, if successful, execution of any court judgment given in reliance upon the adjudicator's award may be stayed pending reversal proceedings pursuant to rules of court.[8]

### 3.2.6  Tort

A claim in tort, eg for negligence against a person with whom the claimant has no contract, cannot be subject to the right to adjudication created by s 108 of the Act even if the claim arises out of construction operations. This is because there is no construction contract between the parties. A claim in tort between parties to a construction contract may fall within the Act if it is a dispute arising 'under' a construction contract for example, if it arises under an express or implied contractual negligence term.[9]

---

4   See *Bowstead and Reynolds on Agency*, para 9-011.
5   See *Bowstead and Reynolds on Agency*, para 9-059.
6   See s 104(3).
7   An assignee takes subject to equities. Cross-claims may in appropriate cases be available against assignees through this medium.
8   RSC Ord 14, r 3(2) or RSC Ord 47, r 1. See *Tubeworkers Ltd v Tilbury Construction Ltd* (1985) 30 BLR 67. This may be so even if the contract contains a restriction on set-off against adjudicator's awards. See Chapter 7.
9   See para 3.5.

---

## 3.3    The right to adjudication

### 3.3.1  Enforcement of the right to adjudicate

There is little benefit in having a right unless it can be enforced. A contractual right to arbitration is enforced not directly but indirectly through a stay of court proceedings brought in contravention of the arbitration agreement. A recalcitrant claimant has the option of pursuing his rights in arbitration or abandoning his claim. In the context of adjudication, the analogy with arbitration is not appropriate. First, a claimant is free to choose his right to litigate as opposed to his right to adjudicate for the resolution of his dispute. It would be entirely inappropriate for a court to grant a stay of court proceedings.[10] Secondly, adjudication under the Act is intended, in the absence of agreement to the contrary, to be of interim effect only pending final resolution of the dispute by other means. It makes little sense to delay the final resolution procedure simply because the interim procedure has not taken place.

### 3.3.2 Enforcement of obligation to adjudicate

If the contract provides for adjudication as an obligation as opposed to merely a right, it is likely that the court will exercise its inherent jurisdiction to stay court proceedings brought in breach of the contract to adjudicate (*Channel Tunnel Group Ltd v Balfour Beatty Ltd* [1993] 2 WLR 262).[11] However, if the right to adjudicate remains a right and not an obligation under the contract, a party with a claim remains free to pursue dispute resolution as he considers appropriate.

### 3.3.3 Appointment procedure—no need to enforce

Co-operation of both parties will usually not be required for the appointment of an adjudicator. If the contract names an adjudicator he may be appointed unilaterally. If the contract names an institution for the nomination of an adjudicator, the institution may be approached unilaterally. It is only if the contract requires co-operation between the parties for the appointment of an adjudicator that one party may, by his failure, refusal or inability to agree upon the appointment of the adjudicator, prevent an adjudicator being appointed. A contract which permits of this potential may be found not to 'provide a timetable with the object of securing the appointment of the adjudicator 'within the prescribed periods as required by s 108(2)(*b*).[12] In this case the Scheme will apply.

### 3.3.4 Other procedural requirements—no need to enforce

If the claimant chooses adjudication as the means of resolving his dispute, and the defending party fails to co-operate, for example, fails to comply with an interlocutory order or fails to attend the hearing, an adjudicator, like an arbitrator, will be free to make his award notwithstanding such lack of co-operation. The award will be binding pursuant to s 108(3) until the dispute is finally determined by court or arbitration proceedings or by agreement. An adjudicator should not make an award in favour of the claimant simply because the defendant has failed to participate in the procedure. He should only find in the claimant's favour if satisfied of the claimant's case. In the unlikely event that it is the claimant who fails to participate in the proceedings, the adjudicator may well have insufficient material upon which to justify a decision in favour of the claimant. In this case, the adjudicator should find for the defendant. The adjudicator should not simply abandon the proceedings. If he does so, the claimant will be free to commence adjudication proceedings afresh with the attendant expense and aggrava-tion for the defendant. The adjudicator is free to take the initiative in ascertain-ing fact and law, so he may, notwithstanding the claimant's or the defendant's failure to co-operate in the conduct of the proceedings, still be able to ascertain fact and law in the defaulting party's favour.[13] There is, however, no equivalent in the context of adjudication of s 41 of the Arbitration Act 1996 which allows the arbitrator to make peremptory orders and enforce them by sanction. Notwith-standing, the adjudicator may proceed to award without co-operation of a party and is probably entitled to draw such adverse inferences as may be appropriate against a party in default of compliance with his orders.

### 3.3.5 Exclusion

If the parties agree that the dispute which has arisen is more appropriate for resolution by, for example, arbitration than adjudication, may an adjudication subsequently be commenced and an award enforced in breach of the exclusion agreement? Section 108 does not prohibit exclusion of its terms.

### 3.3.6 Exclusion in construction contract

If no right to adjudication is provided in the construction contract or, if provided and excluded by the same contract, the provisions of s 108(2)–(4) cannot be said to be satisfied and, in consequence, pursuant to s 108(5), the Scheme will apply.

### 3.3.7 Exclusion after dispute arises

The above reasoning does not apply to exclusion agreements made after the con-struction contract is concluded. The only 'sanction' for failing to make provision complying with s 108(1)–(4) is the applicability of the Scheme. The Scheme ap-plies only 'if the contract does not comply with the requirements of subss (1)–(4).[14] If the contract does so comply, the Scheme does not apply, and this is so even if the right conferred by s 108(1) has subsequently been excluded by agree-ment. However, it is arguable that any contractual attempt to exclude the right to adjudication will be void—contractual exclusions of statutory rights are gener-ally ineffective.

---

10 This is so even if the other party wishes to adjudicate. He may do so notwithstanding concur-rent court proceedings. The adjudicator does not have sole jurisdiction.
11 Possibly also in appropriate cases under s 9 of the Arbitration Act 1996, pursuant to the reason-ing in *Channel Tunnel Group Ltd (above)*.
12 See para **4.2.11**.
13 An arbitrator will often not have this freedom. See *Fox v Wellfair* 19 BLR 52 where the court stressed that it was no part of the arbitrator's function to protect the interests of a defendant who failed to attend the hearing. Finding in the defendant's favour on the basis of material that had not been put before him by one of the parties and not allowing the claimant comment was condemned. See para **4.3.2**.
14 Section 108(5).

## 3.4    Dispute or difference

### 3.4.1    Any dispute

Under s 108(1) 'a dispute' may be referred for adjudication. In the first draft of the Bill, the corresponding words were 'any dispute', but it is unlikely that the change to 'a dispute' has any significance. The Act was intended to create a right to adjudication in respect of any dispute of any nature arising under the contract. It was felt that to define the types of disputes to which the right of adjudication applied would create the opportunity for disagreement as to the jurisdiction of the adjudicator to hear the particular dispute in fact referred to him. The right to adjudication created by s 108 is, therefore, not limited to disputes arising prior to completion of the works or to disputes about time, money, set-off or any other matter.

There is no merit in listing disputes which fall within the rubric of 'a dispute'. However, the following will, subject to what appears below, be included: disputes relating to delay, disruption, valuation of variations, payments due, extensions of time, the right to set-off, the entitlement to issue variations, the entitlement to assign, the right to terminate, the right to suspend, allegations of poor quality workmanship, allegations of defective design, other allegations of professional negligence or misconduct, alleged acceleration agreements and even allegations of fraud.

### 3.4.2    No dispute

There is significant authority on the meaning of 'dispute or difference'. Much of it arises on the application of one party for a stay of court proceedings brought in contravention of an arbitration agreement. For reasons given previously,[15] applications to stay court proceedings to adjudication will be less common than applications to stay court proceedings to arbitration. The argument that there is no dispute or difference which could be referred to arbitration because one party's case is indisputably good or the other's indisputably bad has been rejected (*Hayter v Nelson and Home Insurance Co* [1990] 2 Lloyd's Rep 265).[16] It is likely that what constitutes a dispute referable to adjudication will not be construed differently.

### 3.4.3    Claim and rejection

A 'dispute' or 'difference' does not exist merely because a party asserts a claim. Still less does it exist before a party asserts a claim. In *Monmouth CC v Costelloe & Kemple Ltd* (1963) LGR 429, the Court of Appeal held that in order for a dispute or difference to have arisen there had to be both a claim and a rejection of it. In *Cruden Construction Ltd v Commission for the New Towns* 75 BLR 134, the claimant notified the defendant that it intended to commence arbitration proceedings for the recovery of a claim, without specifying the claim and without giving the defendant the opportunity to accept or reject it. The court held that no dispute or difference had arisen within the meaning of the arbitration clause in question, and the arbitration was improperly (and invalidly) commenced. This was notwithstanding that there was, in this case, every reason to believe that had the defendant been given details of the claim and the opportunity to accept or reject it, it would almost certainly have rejected it in the first instance. The court did not shy away from the practical consequence of this decision which was that the claim may have become time barred for the commencement of arbitration afresh.

### 3.4.4   No cause of action need have arisen

A difference between parties which does not result from an accrued cause of action may fall within the scope of an agreement to refer a dispute or difference to adjudication. It has been said in the context of arbitration that parties may agree to have a dispute decided before the question of legal liability has arisen by actual breach of contract (*JF Robertson & Co v AT James & Co* (1923) 16 Lloyd's Rep 430). Differences as to the construction of contracts the resolution of which will do no more than inform the parties of their contractual rights and obligations will be referable to adjudication under s 108. An arbitrator may have power to crystallise substantive rights under the contract by, for example, filling a gap left in the contract with his view of what is reasonable (*F&G Sykes (Wessex) Ltd v Fine Fare Ltd* [1967] 1 Lloyd's Rep 53; see also *Northern Regional Health Authority v Derek Crouch Construction Ltd* [1984] 2 WLR 676). There is no reason why such power should not also be conferred upon an adjudicator.

### 3.4.5   Crystallising a dispute

The conclusion that a dispute resolution procedure has been improperly commenced by reason of the non-existence of a dispute or difference will be rare. A dispute will often have crystallised by correspondence between the parties in more or less precise terms. It is unlikely that a party can prevent a dispute arising by silence or refusal to deal substantively with a claim. Once a reasonable time for acceptance of the claim has passed continued silence will probably amount to implied rejection of the claim thus conferring jurisdiction upon the adjudicator to resolve the dispute.

There is no reason why the contract should not provide a procedure for crystallising a dispute. It may, for example, specify a time within which a claim must be answered failing which a dispute will be deemed to have arisen. Care should be taken in the drafting of such provision to ensure that it is not in effect a restriction upon the time when a dispute may be referred to adjudication. There is a conceptual distinction between a contractual provision which allows one party a specified period of time within which to formulate his response to a claim made by the other and one which disallows the commencement of adjudication until after a specified period of time. In the former case, the clause defines when the dispute arises. In the latter case, the clause is a restriction upon the time when a dispute may be referred to adjudication, in contravention of s 108(2)(*a*).

### 3.4.6   Certificates

Under many construction contracts, standard form and bespoke, certain of the parties' rights (eg the right to interim and final payment and the right to an extension of time) are to be ascertained by a third party, usually a professional engaged in the project, such as the architect or engineer. The determination of these rights, usually in the form of certificates, opinions or decisions, may or may not have contractual status, and the person making the determination, the certifier, may be exercising a merely administrative role or may be the procedure by which the substantive rights and obligations under the contract are to be ascertained.[17] Many construction contracts also contain arbitration provisions which expressly enable the arbitrator to 'open up, review and revise' certificates.

### 3.4.7   *Northern Regional Health Authority v Derek Crouch Construction Ltd* (1984) 2 WLR 676

In *Crouch*[18] the Court of Appeal denied the courts the power to review certificates issued in circumstances where, on proper analysis, the contract confers upon such third party certifier power to make substantive determination of rights. Where the parties had by their contract agreed that a particular person was to determine their substantive rights, a court would not substitute its own view as to those rights, as to do so would mean that the court was not enforcing the contract, but re-writing it. It has been held in a number of cases[19] that the courts have no jurisdiction to review a certifier's decision, even in the absence of an arbitration clause conferring express power to open up, review and revise certificates. Thus, in *Crouch* the role of the certifier was held to be analogous to that of a valuer under many types of contract, whereby the parties agree to be bound finally by the determination of a third party.

### 3.4.8   *Beaufort Developments (NI) Ltd v Gilbert-Ash (NI) Ltd and Others* (House of Lords, 20 May 1998)

In this case, the decision of the Court of Appeal in *Crouch* was overturned. The principle that a court would not re-write the parties' contract was not impugned and contracts such as contracts for the sale of property at a valuation to be determined by a named person as expert were not questioned. However, the House of Lords did not believe that the language and background of the contract there under consideration[20] suggested that any certificate other than the final certificate was intended to have conclusive effect. In these circumstances, for the courts to have the power to open up, review and revise interim certificates, it was not necessary for the contract specifically to confer such power. The power already existed as part of the courts' ordinary power to enforce the contract in accordance with its terms.[21]

The decision in *Beaufort* is likely to have effects which are more practical than theoretical. In theoretical terms, the reasoning in *Crouch* has not been overturned. If a contract does confer power on a third party to ascertain conclusively substantive rights, then the court has no power to revise that ascertainment. *Beaufort* does not obviate the need to scrutinise each contract in order to ascertain whether the certifier was intended by the parties conclusively to ascertain the parties' rights. However, it is likely that in the light of the decision in *Beaufort* the courts will be less ready to find that the parties did so intend and will approach their task of interpreting the contract for this purpose from a presumption that they not did.

### 3.4.9   What it means for adjudication

Neither *Crouch* nor *Beaufort* were concerned with an adjudicator's powers. An adjudicator is required to apply the applicable law (including the contract) to the facts of the dispute as ascertained by him and make a decision accordingly.[22] If, notwithstanding the decision in *Beaufort*, a certificate issued under the contract is, on proper construction, conclusive as being the determination of a third party vested by the parties with the authority to ascertain substantive rights, the adjudicator has no more power than a court to review and revise it. However, following the decision in *Beaufort*, it is more likely that the contract will not, properly construed, be held to have this effect and an adjudicator, like a court, will have power to open up, review and revise interim certificates.

This result may have onerous implications for the parties to construction contracts and may result in numerous and vexatious attacks on interim certificates with a view to improving cash flow or exerting pressure on one party to make additional payments in the desire to avoid the expense and inconvenience of adjudication.

### 3.4.10   Conclusivity

If it is accepted that the adjudicator must apply the law of the contract to the facts of the dispute, it follows that a contractual provision that in stated events a matter arising under the contract becomes conclusively resolved is binding upon the parties and is not subject to review by an adjudicator. For example, issue of final certificate under clause 30.9 JCT 1963[23] (and other similar provisions) is conclusive as to the matters set out in that clause (see, for example, *Crown Estate Commissioners v John Mowlem & Company Ltd* (1994) 70 BLR 1). There is no reason why an adjudicator should have greater power to override the contractually agreed conclusivity than a court.

### 3.4.11   Restriction or exclusion of disputes referable to adjudication

A contractual clause which excludes certain disputes from the right to adjudication, for example, a dispute involving allegations of fraud, or one which limits the right to adjudication, for example, to disputes concerning the quantum of a claim or the construction of a contract will be non-compliant with s 108 with the result that the Scheme will apply.

### 3.4.12   Effect of restriction or exclusion

If the contract excludes from the adjudication procedure certain types of dispute the Scheme will be applicable to all disputes arising under the contract and not just those excluded. Section 108(5) renders the Scheme applicable 'if the contract does not comply with the requirements of subsections (1)–(4)'. One of the requirements to be met is that a party to a construction contract has the right to refer 'a dispute' (ie any dispute) to adjudication. If this is not achieved, the Scheme will apply. The wording of the Act does not contemplate the applicability of the Scheme *pro-tanto*. This result is justified by the desirability of avoiding room for argument between the parties as to whether a dispute is or is not excluded from the contractual adjudication procedure and therefore whether it or the Scheme applies. There should be no room for question as to the appropriate procedure to follow if the dispute gives rise to some issues which are included within the contractual adjudication procedure and some which are excluded. It is a more satisfactory solution that the Scheme should apply to all disputes arising under the contract or that it should apply to none.

---

17 The provisions of each contract must be closely scrutinised in order to ascertain whether the parties did in fact confer power upon the certifier to determine their substantive rights.
18 The contract there considered was JCT 63, Private with Quantities.
19 See, for example, *Oram Builders Ltd v MJ Pemberton* (1984) 29 BLR 23 where it was said of Crouch: 'The Court of Appeal was accordingly of the opinion not that the arbitration clause deprived the court of jurisdiction but rather that it gave to the arbitrator a jurisdiction to open up, review and revise certificates which the court did not possess'. See also *Balfour Beatty Ltd v Docklands Light Railway* CILL April 1996 1143. In *Reid v Van der Vorm* (1985) 35 BLR 136 His Honour Judge Lewis Hawsher QC was satisfied that the decision in *Crouch* applied even in the absence of any arbitration clause at all.
20 JCT 80 Private Without Quantities.
21 It is beyond the scope of this book to attempt an analysis of the wider implications of the decision in *Beaufort Developments (NI) Ltd to Gilbert-Ash NI Ltd and Others* (House of Lords, 20 May 1998).
22 See para **4.4**.
23 Private with Quantities.

---

## 3.5   Under the contract

It is only if a dispute arises 'under the contract' that the parties to the contract have the statutory right to adjudication. The parties may, by their contract, extend the circumstances in which the right to adjudication arises. So, the contract may provide the right to adjudication in relation to any dispute 'arising under, out of or in connection with' the contract. The contract must not restrict the right to adjudication. So, if the contract provides a right to adjudication only for disputes concerning the construction of the contract, the contract will be non-compliant with s 108. Each individual dispute and each individual contract must be construed carefully to ascertain whether the dispute arises 'under the contract'. Authority in previous cases as to whether a dispute arises 'under the contract' and as to the scope of the clauses there considered are not binding in subsequent cases. They are of persuasive authority only (*Ashville Investments*

*Ltd v Elmer Contractors Ltd* [1989] QB 488). The authorities discussed in this section have arisen in the context of arbitration and foreign jurisdiction clauses. It is likely that a similar construction will apply in the context of adjudication.

### 3.5.1 Disputes as to existence of contract

A dispute as to whether a valid contract ever came into existence and if so whether it contained enforceable adjudication provisions cannot be a dispute over which an adjudicator has ultimate jurisdiction as the existence of such contract is, pursuant to s 108, a pre-condition for the adjudicator's jurisdiction. So, issues concerning whether a contract was void *ab initio*, fails for lack of consideration or was ever concluded at all cannot be conclusively resolved by the adjudicator such as to foreclose from subsequent review by a court the question of the adjudicator's jurisdiction to decide the substantive dispute. Often, however, the adjudicator should rule upon his own jurisdiction leaving the parties free in subsequent proceedings to take issue with his ruling. Disputes as to subsequent voidability or enforceability may be within the adjudicator's jurisdiction as may apparently disputes as the initial validity of a contract in circumstances where illegality is pleaded (*Harbour Assurance Co (UK) v Kansa General International Insurance Co* [1993] 1 Lloyds Rep 455).

### 3.5.2 Disputes following termination of contract

Where a contract to which s 108 applies was validly formed, but has subsequently been discharged (whether by agreement, breach or frustration) the adjudicator may, by analogy with the position in arbitration, retain jurisdiction to decide disputes arising thereunder, including damages for wrongful repudiation (*Heyman v Darwins* [1942] AC 356)[24]. If so, the adjudicator, whose powers evolve from the contract, will be able to make a decision in relation to disputes arising under that contract even after discharge. It is suggested that the analogy with arbitration in this context is appropriate.

### 3.5.3 Disputes arising 'under' the contract

There is a great deal of authority upon the scope of arbitration agreements which apply to disputes arising 'out of', 'in connection with', 'in relation to', 'in respect of', 'with regard to', 'during the execution of' and 'under' a contract. There is no reason, save a possible judicial anxiety to maximise the effect of s 108, to believe that these words will be construed differently in the context of the right to adjudicate. A clause referring disputes arising 'out of', 'in respect of' or 'in connection with' the contract is probably of wider scope than one referring disputes arising 'under' the contract. The authorities have drawn a distinction between the wider formulation and the narrower formulation (*Government of Gibraltar v Kenney* [1956] 2 QB 410; *Woolf v Collis Removal Services* [1948] 1 KB 11; *Antonis P Lemos* [1985] 1 AC 711 at p 727; *Ethiopian Oil Seeds & Pulses Export Corp v Rio Del Mar Foods Inc* [1990] 1 Lloyd's Rep 86; *The Paola D'Alesio* [1994] 2 Lloyds Rep 366. See, however, *The Evje* [1974] 2 Lloyd's Rep 57). The distinction is one drawn not only by lawyers but by the parties also (*Overseas Union Insurance v AA Mu-*

*tual International Insurance Ltd* [1988] 2 Lloyd's Rep 62 per Evans J at p 67). Many decisions on clauses which include both formulations restrict discussion to the wider formulation. Thus authority on the narrower formulation is limited. In *Government of Gibraltar v Kenney* [1956] 2 QB 410 it was said by Sellers J that it is clear that 'arising out of' is 'very much wider' a formulation than arising 'under' the agreement. The authorities are not decided on this issue (*The Evje* [1974] 2 Lloyd's Rep 57), but it is suggested that as a matter of plain English 'under' is a more restricted formulation than many other formulations such as 'in connection with' or 'in respect of'.

In *Heyman v Darwins* [1942] AC 356 an arbitration clause referring to arbitration disputes arising 'in respect of' the agreement or out of it was held to be sufficiently widely drafted to include disputes as to breach, repudiation and frustration of the contract. It was said that such disputes would also fall within the scope of an arbitration clause which refers to arbitration disputes arising 'under' the contract. Disputes arising as to the construction of the contract, whether one party is in breach (including breach of implied terms) and the consequences thereof will arise 'under the contract'.

### 3.5.4   Disputes not arising under the contract

In *Fillite (Runcorn) Ltd v Aqua Lift* 45 BLR 27 it was said that disputes concerning misrepresentation, negligent misstatement or collateral undertakings did not fall within the submission of disputes arising 'under the contract' as this phraseology was not wide enough to include disputes which did not concern obligations created by or incorporated into the contract. The following are probably not disputes arising 'under' the contract:

(1)   Claims for negligent or fraudulent misrepresentation inducing the contract.
(2)   Tortious claims such as for defamation, negligent misstatement, misrepresentation under s 2(1) of the Misrepresentation Act 1967, nuisance etc. Claims for contractual negligence will often be claims 'under the contract' as they arise from express or implied terms of the contract.
(3)   Restitutionary claims and claims based upon trusts. Claims for the creation of trust funds, for example for retention, under specific terms of the contract may give rise to disputes arising 'under' the contract.
(4)   Claims arising under variations to the contract and collateral undertakings and agreements (*The Evje* [1974] 2 Lloyd's Rep 57).
(5)   Claims for breach of statutory duty. Statutory obligations which are incorporated into the contract may give rise to claims 'under the contract'.

---

24   See also s 7 of the Arbitration Act 1996.

---

## 3.6   Compliant procedure

It was seen in Chapter 1 that there is no statutory or judicial definition of adjudication. Section 108(2)–(4) sets out a procedure to be followed and calls it adjudication. Therefore, for the purposes of the Act, the requirements of that section define what amounts to adjudication. Chapter 4 deals with the procedural requirements of s 108(2)–(4) of the Act.

# 4

# The Procedural
# Requirements of the Act

## 4.1 Introduction

Section 108(2)–(4) of the Act sets out the procedural requirements to be met by the contract if the Scheme is to be avoided. It contains only the most skeletal detail. The parties are free to reach agreement on other aspects of adjudication. The procedural requirements of s 108(2)–(4) will be dealt with in this chapter in five sections: timetable, duty to act impartially, power to take the initiative, immunity from suit and the interim binding nature of the award.

## 4.2 Timetable

### 4.2.1 Compliant timetable

By s 108(2)(*a*)–(*d*), the Act sets out requirements as to the time within which the adjudicator must be appointed, the dispute referred to him and his decision reached. The detail as to how these timetables are to be achieved is left for the parties to agree. If the Scheme is to be avoided, a timetable must be agreed with a view to achieving the objectives of s 108(2). It is not sufficient that the parties provide that the objectives of s 108(2) should be met if there is no mechanism for meeting them.

### 4.2.2 Mandatory or maximum time periods

There is no guidance in the Act as to whether the time periods required to be provided in the contract are maximum or mandatory periods. In no case will a contractual adjudication provision which lengthens the statutory time periods be compliant with s 108. A contractual adjudication scheme which shortens the statutory time periods may be compliant with s 108 if those periods are maximum and not mandatory periods. The wording of s 108(2) appears mandatory in nature ('the contract shall …'). However, it is arguable that a contract which provides shorter limits than those appearing in the Act complies with s 108 on the principle that the greater includes the lesser. The safest course in the absence of authority is for the contract to specify the periods stated in the Act and assume they are mandatory.

### 4.2.3  Commencement of adjudication

The timetable to be met in compliance with s 108 of the Act is short. In the absence of an extension of this timetable which may only be made in the limited circumstances specified by the Act, the time from the commencement of the procedure to the adjudicator reaching his decision should not exceed 35 days. This period of 35 days commences upon service of notice by the claimant. It is within the claimant's power to defer the commencement of the procedure until such time as his case for the adjudication is fully prepared. He may then be in a position to ambush an unprepared defendant.

### 4.2.4  Notice

By s 108(2)(a) it is required that the contract shall enable a party to give notice at any time of his intention to refer a dispute to adjudication. The Act does not specify to whom such notice must be given. However, the contract should make provision enabling notice to be given to the other party to the dispute (or his agent). There is no need to give notice to all parties to the contract if they are not involved in the adjudication.

### 4.2.5  Form of notice

No particular form of notice is prescribed and it is not expressly required that the notice be in writing. Section 115(1) of the Act states that the parties are free to agree (but does not require them to agree) on the manner of service of any notice or other document required or authorised to be served for the purposes of the Act. This section assumes that notice will be in writing. Section 115(6) provides that reference to a notice includes any form of communication in writing. It does not expressly provide that reference to a notice includes only forms of communication in writing such as to exclude communications not in writing. It is arguable that it does so by implication. Notice triggers the valid commencement of adjudication, so a party seeking adjudication would be wise to give notice in writing.

### 4.2.6  Content of notice

Whilst no specified form of notice is required under s 108(2)(a), the notice must in fact specify the intention to refer the dispute to adjudication. The threat to refer a dispute to adjudication if a claim is not met will not be sufficient to bring about the commencement of the adjudication procedure. The notice to be served under s 108(2)(a) is the event which sets the adjudication procedure in motion and conditional, vague or ambivalent references to an adjudication procedure at some time in the future will probably not be capable of this effect (*Darlington BC v Waring & Gillow (Holdings) Ltd* (1988) 45 EG 102).

The notice must specify the dispute which is in fact subsequently referred. It is probably not sufficient that the notice refers to 'a' dispute without specifying what that dispute is. A general formulation of the dispute will be sufficient. Care must be taken in the formulation of the dispute referred. If the dispute is incorrectly formulated, the adjudicator may decide the wrong issue. He will have no jurisdiction to decide the right issue (*The Massalia* [1959] 2 Lloyd's Rep 1).

### 4.2.7 Time of notice

The notice under s 108(2)(*a*) may be given 'at any time'. The adjudication procedure is not limited to disputes arising before completion of the contract and therefore a dispute may be adjudicated years after completion of the project. The contract should not restrict the time for service of a notice of intention to refer a dispute to adjudication, for example, by conditioning adjudication upon prior conciliation[1] or reference to some other decision maker.[2] Notice may be given under s 108(2)(*a*) even after the expiry of the limitation period for the cause of action referred or after the issue referred to adjudication has, pursuant to the contract, become conclusive.[3] However, it is ordinarily the obligation of the adjudicator to apply the law of the contract to the facts of the dispute and the claim should fail (by analogy with arbitration see *Re Astley & Tyldesley Coal & Salt Co* (1889) 68 LJQB 252; *Board of Trade v Cayzer Irvine & Co* [1927] AC 610). If, contrary to the law, it succeeds, unless the adjudicator can be shown to have acted without jurisdiction there will often be little redress for the aggrieved party save the commencement of court or arbitration proceedings to overturn the award (see Chapter 7).

### 4.2.8 Appointment of adjudicator and referral of dispute

Section 108(2)(*b*) requires the contract to provide a timetable with the object of securing the appointment of the adjudicator and the referral of the dispute to him within seven days of the notice given under s 108(2)(*a*). Both the appointment of the adjudicator and the referral of the dispute must be catered for within the timetable set by s 108(2)(*b*). The Act gives no guidance upon what constitutes 'appointment' and 'referral of the dispute'.

### 4.2.9 Time for appointment of adjudicator

It is probably the case that the 'appointment' of the adjudicator does not occur until the parties have accepted an adjudicator (either by the terms of the contract or by agreement after the dispute has arisen) or he has been nominated by a procedure in accordance with the contract, the proposed adjudicator has agreed to act and the parties have been notified accordingly (*Tradax Export SA v Volkswagenwerk* [1970] 1 Lloyd's Rep 62; see also *Tew v Harris* (1847) 11 QB 7). If this is so, non-acceptance by one of the parties of the adjudicator's terms may seriously disrupt the proceedings. If the parties (or one of them) do not accept the adjudicator's terms, the adjudicator may decline to act. A recalcitrant party has scope to thwart or at least delay the proceedings.

It is within the claimant's power to minimise the effect of such tactics. Most adjudicators will be persuaded to act if they have satisfactory undertakings as to their fees and immunity from suit. As regards fees, one party may pay or agree to pay the adjudicator's fees and seek to recover them or part of them from the other as part of the adjudicator's award or as a debt.[4] As regards immunity from suit, the adjudicator may enjoy immunity from suit at common law (*Arenson v Casson Beckman* Rutley & Co [1975] 3 WLR 815) or one party may give the adjudicator an indemnity against any liability which the adjudicator may incur which the other has not agreed to waive.[5] In this case, he may be entitled to have any action against the adjudicator stayed or dismissed (*Gore v Van der Lann* [1967] 2 QB 31; *Snelling v John Snelling Ltd* [1973] 1 QB 87).

Alternatively, he may be able to recover from the defaulting party as damages for breach of contract sums paid out under the indemnity.

An alternative which is perhaps less attractive is available where the contractual adjudication machinery has broken down. In this case the court may intervene. This is an unsatisfactory result as the need for court intervention will inevitably delay the adjudicator's decision. In the context of expert determination where one party refused to appoint a valuer as required by the contract the court intervened not to appoint a valuer for him but to ascertain the very issue which the expert was to determine (*Sudbrook Trading Estates Ltd v Eggleton* [1983] AC 444). Such a procedure would provide little comfort to a party anxious to have his dispute determined in adjudication quickly and by an individual chosen for his expertise. The court probably has power to appoint an adjudicator on terms set out in the construction contract (*Sudbrook Trading Estates Ltd v Eggleton* [1983] AC 444).

### 4.2.10 Terms of adjudicator's appointment

If the parties enter into a formal contract with the adjudicator, that contract will govern the relationship of all parties. It may or may not, upon its proper construction, incorporate relevant terms from the construction contract. It is suggested that it will ordinarily do so unless such terms were clearly intended to be excluded. If the parties do not enter into a formal contract with the adjudicator, his relationship with them (or at least the claimant[6]) may be analysed as an implied contract subject to implied terms. If this analysis is not possible on the facts of any particular case, the adjudicator's rights and obligations will be ascertained in accordance with the general law.[7]

### 4.2.11 Method of appointing adjudicator

If an adjudicator is to be named in the contract, the parties would be wise to ascertain from the proposed nominee his willingness to act when the need arises. The contract should also provide some alternative procedure for the appointment of an adjudicator to cater for the possibility that the named adjudicator is unable or unwilling to act, for instance, because of previous commitments or by reason of a recent interest in one of the parties. In the absence of such alternative appointment procedure an adjudicator can be appointed only by application to court (*Sudbrook Trading Estates Ltd v Eggleton* [1983] AC 444). In such circumstances, there will be no effective right to adjudication within the timescales envisaged by the Act and the contract may be held to be non-compliant with s 108 such that the Scheme applies. A proposed adjudicator should ensure, when agreeing to nomination in a contract, that his agreement is not in fact an agreement to act. If the proper construction of the agreement is that he has undertaken to act as adjudicator he may be in breach of contract with the parties if, when a dispute arises, prior commitments render him unable to honour his undertaking. In this event, he may be entitled to no immunity from suit in respect of the consequences of his breach.[8] The breach probably does not arise from acts or omissions in the 'discharge or purported discharge' of his functions as adjudicator—if he is unable to act he may not have been constituted adjudicator.

If the contract does not name an adjudicator it must 'provide a timetable' with the object of securing his appointment. This may involve appointment of an adjudicator by agreement between the parties, by nomination of one of the parties, by a nominating institution[9] or by some other procedure. If the contract leaves appointment of the adjudicator for agreement by the parties, it should provide a mechanism for nomination of an adjudicator in default of agreement. In the absence of such default nomination procedure, one party may, by his failure or refusal to agree an adjudicator, thwart the statutory right to adjudication. A contract permitting of this potential may be non-compliant with s 108. The contract should provide for the default nomination procedure to be complete and the dispute referred within seven days of the notice of intention to refer. This leaves little time for the parties to attempt to reach agreement.

### 4.2.12 Referral of dispute

The timetable set out in the contract must have the object of securing the 'referral of the dispute' to the adjudicator within seven days of the notice of intention to refer served under s 108(2)(a). The Act does not specify what constitutes 'referral' of the dispute. The parties may, by their contract, make such provision in this regard as they see fit such as for example that the referral must be in writing, must not exceed a stated length and must append all documents and/or the statements of witnesses relied on. A dispute may involve not only a claim which is rejected, but possibly also (or only) a cross-claim. The power to refer a 'dispute' to adjudication is not the same as the power to refer a 'claim' to adjudication. If the defendant accepts the claim but raises a cross-claim which is not accepted, it is the cross-claim and not the claim which is in dispute.[10] The claimant probably has the right to refer to adjudication a 'dispute' arising under the contract, including one arising upon a cross-claim.[11] If the claimant refers to adjudication only his uncontested claim, the adjudicator will have no jurisdiction to make an award on it as it is not in dispute (*The Massalia* [1959] 2 Lloyd's Rep 1; *The Kostas Melas* [1981] 1 Lloyd's Rep 18 at p 25; see also Chapter 7).

### 4.2.13 Formulation of the dispute referred

The adjudicator has jurisdiction to decide only the dispute in fact referred to him and not another dispute that ought to have been referred to him.[12] Care must therefore be taken in formulating the dispute referred for, while it is unlikely that either adjudicator or court reviewing the proceedings will take a meticulous approach to the precise definition of the dispute referred to adjudication, in each case the broad formulation of the dispute referred will define the extent of the adjudicator's jurisdiction. It is probably the case that a counterclaim, not amounting to set-off, can often not be raised in the adjudication proceedings. This is because a counterclaim not amounting to set-off is not a defence to the claim but is a separate and independent claim which will often not have been the subject of the referral to adjudication. It will, therefore, be outside the adjudicator's jurisdiction. In the absence of agreement to the contrary, the adjudicator's jurisdiction extends only to disputes in existence at the time of referral

### 4.2.14 Time for the adjudicator to reach his decision

By s 108(2)(c) the contract is to require the adjudicator to reach a decision within 28 days of referral of the dispute or such longer period as is permitted pursuant to the Act. The adjudicator has therefore a period of 28 days within which to conduct the procedures prescribed by the contract, take the initiative in ascertaining the facts and the law and reach a decision. Section 108(2)(c) does not require that the adjudicator communicate his decision to the parties within 28 days. This is the period for reaching his decision. He may be entitled to exercise a *lien* over his decision for payment of his fees.

### 4.2.15 Extensions of time

Section 108(2) enables the contract to allow the period of 28 days to be extended in two circumstances:

(1)  Under s 108(2)(c) by agreement between the parties after the dispute has been referred. Extension of the period of 28 days before referral of the dispute is not permitted. If it were permitted in the underlying construction contract, a stronger contracting party may impose a very long extension of time upon a weaker one thereby defeating the objectives of the Act. There is no limit on the length of extension that may be agreed under s 108(2)(c) after the dispute has been referred.

(2)  By the adjudicator with the consent of the claimant by up to 14 days under s 108(2)(d). An extension of time under this section should be at the instigation of the adjudicator and not the claimant. In practice, this will be almost impossible to police. Consent of the defendant is not required.

There is no restriction upon how extensions of time may be used, whether for submission, investigation, deliberation or some combination of all of these and it is therefore for the parties and/or the adjudicator to make such provision as they or he see(s) fit.

### 4.2.16 Adjudicator unable to reach a decision

The period of 28 days for the adjudicator to reach a decision may be insufficient to enable him to decide the more complex disputes arising under construction contracts. The adjudicator may not in the time available be able to hear or investigate the facts of the dispute and research the law in all the detail that would be available to a court or arbitrator. He must make a decision on what is available. The mere fact that the adjudicator is not satisfied that he has exhaustively analysed the issues in dispute should not usually prevent him from reaching a decision. There may, however, be some circumstances in which the adjudicator cannot form a view on any rational basis on the material and in the time available to him. The extent to which this occurs will depend upon the nature of the disputes that the construction industry refers to adjudication and the attitudes of individual adjudicators.

If the adjudicator is unable to reach a decision on the merits of the dispute it is suggested that it is not a valid adjudicator's decision with interim binding effect under s 108(3) if the adjudicator were to 'decide' that he is unable to reach a conclusion on the substantive merits of the dispute. Section 108 creates the right to refer a dispute for adjudication in accordance with the procedure set out in that section. It cannot have been intended by the legislature that failure to make a substantive decision could be a 'decision' under s 108. It is mere semantics to say that the adjudicator has reached a 'decision'; namely, that he cannot decide. Presumably the practical result of such a 'decision' would be that the claimant fails and the defendant succeeds on that adjudication. This result should follow but in consequence of more positive reasoning. It should not follow that the claimant is free to shop around in the hope of finding an adjudicator willing to find for him on the substantive merits of the dispute.[13]

### 4.2.17 Interim regulation orders

An adjudicator unable to resolve the substantive dispute, has no power, unless expressly or impliedly conferred by the contract, or by the parties, to make an order for the interim regulation of the parties' positions. He has no power to order that disputed sums be paid into a stakeholder account pending final resolution of the dispute. He has no power to reach a decision on the balance of convenience or to reflect his view as to how the dispute should, in the interests of fairness or commercial reasonableness, best lie unless and until the dispute is finally resolved. The adjudicator is under an obligation to resolve the dispute by applying the law of the contract to the facts of the dispute. An order such as above does not do this. In *The Kostas Melas* [1981] 1 Lloyd's Rep 18, it was said that since the jurisdiction of an arbitrator is to decide matters in dispute between the parties, the power to make an award is a power to decide those matters in dispute. In the absence of some special agreement between the parties, a submission of disputes to arbitration will not generally give the arbitrator the power to order that one party pay a sum to another unless the arbitrator decides that that sum is due and owing. An adjudicator, by reason of the nature of adjudication envisaged by the Act and in particular the very short timetables imposed by s 108, may have a lower threshold of satisfaction as to whether a sum is due and owing. Nevertheless, he should not, in the absence of agreement of the parties to the contrary, award any sum on any basis other than that he believes, in so far as he has been able to ascertain in the time and on the material available, that that sum is due and owing. To the extent that interim preservation orders may be made either in court or in arbitration without agreement of the parties the power to make such order exists only by statute—there is none applicable to adjudication. It is within the parties' power to confer upon the adjudicator such authority in this regard as they see fit including the power to act as 'aimable compositeur'.[14] If they do so, they should specify whether the adjudicator may exercise such authority in the first instance or only after having tried to resolve the dispute by analysis of the parties' legal entitlements.

### 4.2.18 'Burden of proof'

If the contract does not confer upon the adjudicator authority of the nature mentioned above, the adjudicator must in reaching his decision apply the law to the facts of the dispute. If he cannot ascertain what the facts are, he should find against the party whose case depends upon the existence of those facts. The requirement to prove on a 'balance of probabilities' in court or arbitration proceedings means that it must be shown by the claimant that it is more likely than not (more than 50 per cent) that the claim is good. In inquisitorial proceedings,[15] it may be inappropriate to talk of the 'burden of proof', as establishment of the case does not depend solely upon proof by the parties but also (and possibly solely) upon investigation by the tribunal. However, simply because the adjudicator has power to take the initiative in ascertaining the facts does not mean that the claimant should succeed in circumstances where the adjudicator is not satisfied—whether by his own investigations or proof by the parties—that the claimant's case is good. If not so satisfied the adjudicator should find for the defendant. It is only where the facts and evidence are evenly balanced or are so complex that no rational decision can be made in the time available that this principle will determine the outcome of the dispute.

### 4.2.19 Periods of reckoning

The timetables prescribed by s 108 are expressed in terms of days. Days means calendar days. Section 116(3) excludes from the period of reckoning Christmas Day, Good Friday and bank holidays under the Banking and Financial Dealings Act 1971. Section 116(2) excludes the date of notice. Only bank holidays are excluded from the periods stated by the Act. If notice under s 108(2)(a) is given immediately prior to the commencement of the building industry's traditional two week Christmas holiday, it is unlikely that the timetable set by the contract will be achieved.

### 4.2.20 Sanction for failure to comply

There is no sanction provided by the Act for failure by one or other party to comply with the provisions of the contract as regards adjudication.[16] The only sanction is for parties who fail to make the required contractual provision in the first place. In this event the Scheme applies.[17]

---

1   ICE, 6th edn, cl 66 conditions arbitration upon prior conciliation; adjudication should not be so conditioned.
2   FIDIC, 4th edn, cl 67 conditions arbitration upon prior referral of the dispute to the Engineer adjudication should not be so conditioned. See, however, amendment made by ICE to cl 66 of 5th & 6th edn and to cl 66 of ICE Design & Construct. This provision is probably consistent with the Act. See, however, para 3.4.5.
3   For example, under JCT 80, cl 30.9.
4   See para 5.2.6–5.2.7.

5   As required in the contract by s 108(4).
6   See paras **5.1.3** and **5.2.1**.
7   See para **5.2.1**.
8   It will be rare that any loss flows from the breach.
9   Most of the bodies responsible for nominating arbitrators will also nominate adjudicators.
10  Set-off is a defence. Thus, a cross-claim amounting to set-off renders the claim contested. This is not the case with a counterclaim (see Chapter 7).
11  If this is so, the claimant is able to require the defendant to advance his claim in a forum, at a time and within a timetable that may suit only the claimant. In court or arbitration proceedings, the defendant in these circumstances would be allowed sufficient time to investigate and prove his case. In adjudication he will have a period of less than 28 days. See para **7.2.9**.
12  *The Massalia* [1959] 2 Lloyd's Rep 1; *The Kostas Melas* [1981] 1 Lloyd's Rep 18 at p 25.
13  See para **7.1.2**.
14  This is the generic description of a clause which enables a decision maker to make his decision on some basis (which should be specified in the contract) other than by reference to the parties' strict legal entitlements.
15  Adjudication proceedings will often be inquisitorial, at least in part.
16  Such failure will amount to breach of contract and the usual rules will apply.
17  For enforcement of the right to adjudicate see para **3.3**. For enforcement of adjudicator's awards see Chapter 7.

## 4.3   Duty to act impartially

### 4.3.1   No necessary analogy with arbitration

Section 108(2)(*e*) requires the contract to impose a duty on the adjudicator to act impartially. The duty to act impartially will apply throughout the proceedings—in the procedural conduct of the adjudication, in investigating, hearing and assessing the evidence and in reaching a decision. Precisely what the duty to act impartially requires in the context of adjudication cannot be said with certainty. The analogy with the duty of an arbitrator to act impartially may be inappropriate. This is because an adjudicator's role and powers are inquisitorial at least in part and may, depending upon what they are held to entail, be very different from those of an arbitrator.

### 4.3.2   Secret evidence

It is axiomatic that in the context of arbitration there should be no hearing in the absence of one of the parties[18] and the arbitrator should not receive secret information. In *Fox v Wellfair* 19 BLR 52 (see also *The Massalia* [1959] 2 Lloyd's Rep 1; *Town and Country Properties v Wiltshier* 44 BLR 109), the defendant was unrepresented at the hearing, but the arbitrator, without giving the claimant any opportunity to comment, reduced the value of the claim in reliance upon his own view of technical matters which was contrary to the evidence given by the claimant's expert witnesses. The arbitrator was removed for misconduct. He should have offered the claimant the opportunity to comment upon and disprove his theory. It was said that the arbitrator's function is 'not to supply evidence for the defendants but to adjudicate upon the evidence given before him'.[19] If he were to use his own special knowledge to provide evidence he would be discarding the role of 'impartial arbitrator' and 'assuming the role of advocate for the defaulting side'.[20] It was said to be contrary to the rule against taking secret evidence if the arbitrator were to act on his own particular knowledge of the case, without recourse to the evidence given by witnesses on either side. The comment in this case about the arbitrator's powers and duties assumes throughout and requires the arbitrator to be conducting adversarial proceedings.

Adjudicators will usually not be conducting purely adversarial proceedings. They are required by statute to be enabled to take the initiative in ascertaining fact and law.[21] It is implicit in this requirement that the adjudicator's own knowledge obtained in the course of his investigations may form the basis of his decision. The principles in *Fox v Wellfair* (*above*) may, in these circumstances, be inappropriate to the adjudication process. From a practical perspective, if the adjudicator must advise the parties of facts (and presumably the law) ascertained by him and give them the opportunity to comment the onus on the adjudicator may be a heavy one. The facts ascertained by him may be complex and the time period for reaching his decision is short. Time may not allow a rigid adherence to the principles in *Fox v Wellfair* (*above*).

### 4.3.3 Duty to act equally between the parties

It may be that the duty to act impartially means little more than a duty to act equally and fairly as between the parties. What is made available to one party should be made available to both. The adjudicator must not offer one party an opportunity which is not offered to the other. He should not make any form of procedural direction upon application of one party, without hearing the other. He should not allow one party to submit argument or evidence without allowing the other party a reply. Whether in any particular instance the adjudicator has failed in his duty to act impartially will depend upon the circumstances of the case. It is suggested, however, that the adjudicator should ordinarily give the parties, in so far as practicable, the opportunity to comment upon the case advanced by the opponent and upon any fact or theory ascertained by him of which they might otherwise be unaware. This is desirable not only to avoid any suspicion by the parties that they have not had a fair hearing but also because the adjudicator, in ascertaining fact and law, will often be better informed if he has had the benefit of an explanation from the parties.

### 4.3.4 Duty to act fairly

There is no express requirement in s 108 that the contract should provide that the adjudicator must act 'fairly' or 'in accordance with the rules of natural justice'. Lord Reid said in *Wiseman v Borneman* [1971] AC 297 that 'natural justice requires that the procedure before any tribunal which is acting judicially shall be fair in all the circumstances and I would be sorry to see this fundamental general principle degenerate into a series of hard and fast rules'. This robust approach to natural justice applies to arbitrators who are 'bound to observe in their proceedings the ordinary rules which are laid down for the administration of justice (*Haigh v Haigh* 1861 SLT 507). They are not required to take a minute view as to the observance of rules of procedure but must 'take account of those principles of justice which it is impossible to disregard' (*Andrews v Mitchell* [1905] AC 78).

### 4.3.5 Robust approach

A similar robust approach can be expected to the adjudicator's duties whether or not he is acting judicially. It is unlikely that any specific formulations of the rules of natural justice or the duty to act fairly, applicable to administrative, judicial or any other kind of tribunal, will be applied rigidly in the context of adjudication. This is because what is fair will depend upon the circumstances in which the issue arises.

Principles of fairness cannot be crystallised once and for always. They will change with time and circumstance. Parties to an adjudication procedure cannot expect that procedure to be conducted as a High Court action.[22] The unavailability of certain procedures[23] will rarely amount to unfairness. What is fair must be considered in the context of the Act and in particular the speedy timetable to be adopted, the requirement that the adjudicator should be enabled to take the initiative in ascertaining the facts and the law and the fact that adjudication will usually be an interim procedure the result of which may be reversed in court or arbitration proceedings.

### 4.3.6 Must the adjudicator be impartial?

There is no express requirement for the adjudicator to be impartial. During the parliamentary debates before the Act was passed, it was discussed whether the Act should disqualify as adjudicator any person involved with the project. It was decided that there may be circumstances where the appropriate person to be appointed adjudicator was involved with the project, for example, as architect or engineer and that such restriction was therefore undesirable.[24]

### 4.3.7 Personal interest

There is no express statutory requirement that the adjudicator should be impartial or independent of the parties, that he should have no financial or other interest in either of them or the outcome of the award or that he should be seen to be independent. It is, however, undesirable for an individual with a personal or professional interest in either of the parties or the outcome of the award to act as adjudicator. Such a person should decline appointment. An adjudicator who has an obvious financial interest in one of the parties or the outcome of the award may find his award easily challenged on the basis of partiality. It is not certain whether he is disqualified from acting or whether his award could be challenged by the parties even in the absence of proof of some behaviour by which he favours one party over the other without justification. If independence or disinterest are characteristics of the adjudicator required by the parties they should put the matter beyond doubt by making express provision in their contract.

---

18  If both parties are offered the opportunity to attend, but one fails without good reason to do so, it is not contrary to the rule against secret evidence for the arbitrator to hold the hearing in his absence. There is now power conferred by the Arbitration Act 1996, s 34 for the arbitrator to exercise inquisitorial powers.
19  *Per* Lord Denning MR at page 61.
20  *Per* Lord Denning MR at page 62.
21  Section 108(2)(*f*).
22  In *Cape Durasteel Ltd v Rosser and Russell Building Services Ltd* (1995) 46 Con LR 75, it was said by His Honour Judge Humphrey Lloyd QC that a procedure which he accepted as adjudication did not give the parties the right to have their dispute resolved 'as fairly' as would a reference to arbitration.

23  Such as an oral hearing and cross-examination. See *Town and Country Properties v Wiltshier* 44 BLR 109.
24  570 HL Official Report, 28 March 1996 (No 70) per Lord Lucas.

## 4.4    Power to take the initiative

There is nothing in the Act or elsewhere to suggest that the adjudicator's role is other than to apply the law of the contract to the facts of the dispute as found by him. Were he to do otherwise, he would effectively be rewriting the parties' contract thereby bringing about an alteration in their substantive legal rights. Section 108(2)(*f*) requires the adjudicator to be empowered to take the initiative in ascertaining the facts and the law. This probably means that the adjudicator may[25] take an inquisitorial rather than an adversarial approach to his role. It does not necessarily mean that the adjudicator is the sole source of relevant fact and law. An inquisitorial approach is adopted neither in the English courts nor, in the absence of express or necessarily implicit provision, in arbitration (see, for example, *Chilton v Saga Holidays* [1986] 1 All ER 841; see also s 34(2)(*g*) of the Arbitration Act 1996). In circumstances where English common law has little experience of inquisitorial proceedings, it is difficult to state with any measure of confidence precisely what s 108(2)(*f*) requires.

### 4.4.1   Ascertaining the facts

The power to take the initiative in ascertaining fact must have some substantive content. In practice, fact will ordinarily be ascertained from documents or witnesses or from inpections, tests or samples. Section 108(2)(*f*) provides no guidance as to whether the adjudicator is entitled to require access to witnesses or documents or is free to conduct his own inspections, tests and samples. This gives rise to the following questions:

(1)  Is there a limit to the adjudicator's powers of investigation?
(2)  Is a contractual restriction on the right of the adjudicator to require access to witnesses or documents, save as advanced on behalf of a party, inconsistent with the requirement in s 108(2)(*f*) as preventing the adjudicator from taking the initiative?

There is no certain answer to these questions. There is nothing in the Act to indicate the limit of the powers of the adjudicator in taking the initiative in ascertaining fact or law. There is nothing in the Act to indicate that there is a limit. There will usually be nothing objectionable about the adjudicator requesting that the parties make available in the proceedings a particular document or category of documents not already relied upon by the parties. Similarly, there will be no objection if the adjudicator wishes to question witnesses in the presence of the parties. It is probably also unobjectionable for the adjudicator to request permission for a site visit with a view to inspecting alleged defects and forming his own view thereon. He may well be justified in conducting his own tests and samples However, the parties may be justifiably concerned if the adjudicator were to make a direct approach to, say, the architect for a report upon the issues raised in the dispute or a third party witness of fact. If, without the knowledge of the parties, the adjudicator attends site to observe the parties and secretly question witnesses his conduct may have overstepped the line of what is acceptable conduct in ascertaining fact. Unfortunately, the Act draws no line and offers no guidance upon where, if at all, the parties may draw it by their contract. The greater the restrictions on the adjudicator's power or the material available to the adjudicator, the more likely the contractual adjudication arrangements are to be held not to enable the adjudicator to take the initiative in ascertaining fact and law with the consequence that s 108(2)(*f*) has not been complied with and the Scheme applies.

### 4.4.2 Inquisitorial tribunals

Tribunals with inquisitorial powers, such as coroners, are usually heavily regulated by statute. The Act, however, provides no guidance as to what 'taking the initiative' means or how far the adjudicator may exercise inquisitorial powers (*Town & Country Properties v Wiltshier* 44 BLR 109; *Fox v Wellfair* (*above*); *Top Shop Estates Ltd v C Danino*[26]). The adjudicator will not always fulfil a role which is entirely inquisitorial. His role may be purely inquisitorial if, for example, a dispute about defective works can be resolved by visual inspection and the application of the adjudicator's personal judgement. However, it will often not be practicable for the parties to leave the adjudicator to ascertain fact and law unaided. Submission, argument and evidence may often be required by the parties and adjudicator alike. Fact may be complex and need oral testimony (including cross-examination) or written submission by way of explanation. The adjudicator may hear submissions of fact and law made by the parties and his inquisitorial role may be restricted in practical terms to calling for certain documents or categories of documents, requiring to hear the evidence of certain witnesses or questioning those witnesses himself. The adjudicator's role in any particular case may be a hybrid between the purely inquisitorial powers often exercised by valuers and the strictly adversarial role required to be undertaken by arbitrators. Care should therefore be taken before concluding that adjudication under the Act is, by reason of the power in s 108(2)(*f*) of the adjudicator to take the initiative in ascertaining fact and law, necessarily an entirely inquisitorial procedure.[27]

### 4.4.3 Ascertaining the law

The adjudicator must have power to take the initiative in ascertaining the law. Often adjudicators will not be lawyers. Even experienced judges and legal arbitrators are more likely to appreciate the legal principles applicable to a dispute if the rival contentions are brought to their attention by submissions of the parties. There may be few non-legal (or even lawyer) adjudicators who feel confident in ascertaining the law within the time available, completely unaided by submissions of the parties. Unless the contract between the parties gives express or implied authority to the adjudicator to delegate a decision or any part of his duties to another, for example a technical expert or a lawyer, he has no authority so to do. However, by analogy with an arbitrator's powers[28] he may consult with and take advice from others providing always that the ultimate decision is his own.

There are two aspects to this issue:

(1)  If the adjudicator, without authority, appoints another person to provide advice in relation to the dispute, he will not be able to recover the fees of that other person from the parties unless his contract with them expressly or by implication permits. The parties should, when drafting the adjudicator's remuneration terms, ensure that if they do not want the additional expense of experts appointed by the adjudicator, they do not agree it expressly or by implication.

(2)  If, on proper analysis, the award in the adjudication proceedings can be said not to be the adjudicator's decision but the decision of some third person appointed by the adjudicator, the award will not be binding. It will not be the decision of the person to whom the parties agreed to refer their dispute (*Jones (M) v Jones (RR)* [1971] 1 WLR 840; see also *Ess v Truscott* [1837] 2 M&W 385).

There is no equivalent in the context of adjucation of s 37 of the Arbitration Act 1996 which, in the absence of agreement of the parties to the contrary, entitles the arbitrator to appoint experts or advisers and recover their costs from the parties as arbitral expenses. The arbitrator must, however, give the parties reasonable opportunity to comment on any information, opinions or advice given by such adviser or expert.

---

25  The adjudicator is not required to take the initiative.

26  In *Top Shop Estates Ltd v C Danino* [1985] EG 1, p 9, the statement by Leggatt J that the function of the arbitrator is not to play the role of Perry Mason is indicative of judicial dislike for the adoption of inquisitorial procedures by arbitrators. How far the adjudicator can follow in the footsteps of Perry Mason is difficult to assess.

27  If adjudication is entirely inquisitorial, it is probably not a judicial process. See para **4.5.4**. However, it is unlikely that the power to take the initiative necessarily renders a procedure entirely inquisitorial. In the context of arbitration, this power sits happily alongside what appear to be purely adversarial procedures. See Arbitration Act 1996, s 34(2)(*f*) and (*g*).

28  See Mustill and Boyd, *Commercial Arbitration*, p 359.

---

## 4.5    Immunity from suit

### 4.5.1    The contract

The contract must provide that the adjudicator is not liable for anything done or omitted in the discharge or purported discharge of his functions as adjudicator unless the act or omission is in bad faith, and that any employee or agent of the adjudicator is similarly protected from liability (s 108(4)). If the contract does not so provide, it is non-compliant with s 108 and the Scheme applies. The Scheme protects the adjudicator from suit.

### 4.5.2    Bad faith

'Bad faith' in an adjudicator will be very rare. 'Bad faith' has been held to mean malice, personal spite, a desire to injure for improper reasons or knowledge of absence of power to make a decision (*Melton Medes Ltd v SIB* [1995] 3 All ER 880). There is a good argument that the adjudicator who considers that his conduct is not subject to any effective review or sanction and in consequence knowingly exceeds his jurisdiction will be guilty of bad faith with the result that he cannot rely upon immunity from suit.

### 4.5.3 No contractual immunity from suit

The adjudicator is entitled to rely upon contractual immunity from suit only if incorporated into his terms of appointment. If for any reason, such immunity from suit does not become a contractually binding term as between the parties and the adjudicator, the adjudicator acquires immunity only if available under the common law or if proceedings commenced against him can be stayed.[29] There is no equivalent in the context of adjudication of s 29 of the Arbitration Act 1996 granting statutory immunity to arbitrators. However if the adjucator acquires no immunity from suit, his position may not be a serious one. It will be uncommon for any loss to be suffered in consequence of the adjudicator's negligence. The adjudication proceedings may be reversed in court or arbitration.

### 4.5.4 Immunity at common law

In *Arenson v Casson Beckman Rutley & Co* [1975] 3 WLR 815, an expert appointed to decide issues referred to him was held to have no immunity from suit as against one of the appointing parties. The analogy with an arbitrator's immunity or that of a person acting in a judicial role was held to be inappropriate. The House of Lords made it clear that each claim to immunity must be considered in the light of the particular procedure conducted by the person claiming immunity. The judicial nature of the function performed was regarded as one of the essential justifications for immunity from suit.[30] A non-exhaustive list of indicia was set out[31] to assist the analysis in any particular case as to whether immunity from suit is justified. These indicia are that there is a formulated dispute or difference, the decision maker is called upon to exercise a judicial function, the parties must, where appropriate, have had the opportunity to present evidence and/or submissions[32] and the parties have agreed to accept the decision.[33] The parties to construction contracts subject to the Act are free to agree procedure within certain parameters set by s 108. The procedure to be followed and the function performed in adjudications will therefore vary from one case to another in marked respects. The parties are free to confer power upon the adjudicator to exercise functions other than simply resolving a dispute.[34] It is suggested that depending upon the powers conferred upon the adjudicator and the powers in fact exercised by him, the adjudication procedure may be a judicial one notwithstanding section 108(2)(f).[35] Whether any particular adjudication is a judicial process depends not so much on the statutory requirements of s108 as on the contractual adjudication provisions made pursuant thereto. Many adjudications will approximate more to a lis inter partes than to the sort of valuation exercise conducted in *Arenson v Casson Beckman*. The fact that the adjudicator may take the initiative in ascertaining fact and law does not necessarily derogate from the judicial nature of the process. Each adjudication must be considered in the light of its own individual circumstances.[36]

### 4.5.5   Non-parties

Non-parties to the adjudicator's appointment cannot usually be said to have granted the adjudicator immunity. In most circumstances, nor will they have any justifiable claim against the adjudicator. However, there are circumstances in which a third party may make a claim against the adjudicator, such as, for example, for inducing a breach of contract or for negligence. Many such cases would fail if taken to trial. Some may succeed. The adjudicator may, notwithstanding the immunity he is intended to enjoy, wish to extend his professional indemnity insurance to cover activities as adjudicator. Alternatively, or in addition, he may wish to take an indemnity from each of the parties against any liability, including liability for legal costs, incurred by him in defending any claim brought by a third party arising out of or in connection with his role in adjudicating their dispute. Such an indemnity should not be limited to circumstances in which the claim succeeds—it is equally required where it fails and the adjudicator is out of pocket in terms of legal costs.

### 4.5.6   Nominating institutions

Immunity from suit under the Act does not extend to nominating institutions. Nor is there any equivalent in the context of adjudication of s 74 of the Arbitration Act 1996 which gives statutory immunity from suit to arbitral and other institutions appointing arbitrators. Many nominating institutions will demand contractual immunity as a condition of nominating an adjudicator. In other cases the institution will not be entitled to immunity but the circumstances in which an action could be maintained against a nominating institution will be few.

### 4.5.7   Adjucator's employees and agents

An adjucator's employee or agent will not often bear personal liability to a party to the adjucation. This is fortunate for the doctrine of privity of contract usually prevents parties to a contract from effectively conferring immunity from suit upon a non party. A simple contractual provision in a construction contract that the adjudicator or his employees or agents should enjoy immunity from suit will not be effective. Equally, provision in the adjudicator's terms of appointment that his employees or agents should be immune from suit will be ineffective. The Act provides no statutory immunity from suit.[37] There is, however, no reason why an action brought in contravention of a contractual undertaking not to sue should not be stayed or dismissed if the principles set out in *Gore v Van Der Lann* [1967] 2 QB 31 and *Snelling v John Snelling* [1973] 1 QB 87 are fulfilled.[38]

There are further legal devices available by which immunity from suit may be conferred upon a third party. It may be possible on the facts of any particular case to find an implied contract with the adjudicator's employees or agents, eg, with a legal or technical expert engaged by the adjudicator with the express agreement of the parties. The artificial device of agency might successfully be used to ensure that the statutory aim of immunity for adjucator and his employees and agents is achieved.[39] This device is, however, artificial and for this reason the courts have shown a reluctance to follow it, relying instead upon strict contractual and agency principles to deny its application outside the context in which it was first employed, namely, the carriage of goods by sea.[40]

---

29  See para **4.2.9**. An adjudicator will not wish to be dependent, for this purpose, upon the willingness of one party to the dispute to take action against the other to bring about a stay of the proceedings against him.
30  Adjudication is a relatively novel procedure. The authorities considering immunity from suit have proceeded on the basis of the distinction between two procedures, namely arbitration (or the quasi arbitral) and expert determination. The novel and individual position of adjudication may result in the boundaries for immunity from suit being re-drawn to accommodate a procedure which does not fit into existing categories.
31  Lord Wheatley, p 830.
32  See also *Re Hopper* [1867] 2 QB 367.
33  Lord Simon of Glaisdale described the nature of a judicial proceeding in similar terms at pp 825–6.
34  See paras **3.4.4**, **3.4.9** and **4.2.17**.
35  See para **4.4.3**. In *Palacath Ltd v Flanagan* [1985] 2 All ER 161, the court recognised that a process may follow some procedures 'typical of the judicial process' but the ultimate test was whether the decision maker was required to act wholly or in part upon the evidence and submissions of the parties or whether he was to act solely on his own expert opinion. The court analysed the contractual obligations of the expert in order to reach its conclusion.
36  See discussion in Mustill and Boyd, *Commercial Arbitration*, pp 224–30.
37  There is no equivalent in the context of adjucation of s 29(1) and (2) of the Arbitration Act 1996.
38  See para **4.2.9**.
39  See *Scruttons Ltd v Midland Silicones Ltd* [1962] AC 446; *NZ Shipping Co Ltd v Satterthwaite & Co Ltd* [1975] AC 154.
40  See for example *Raymond Burke Motors Ltd v Mersey Docks and Harbour Co* [1986] 1 Lloyds Rep 154; *Southern Water Authority v Carey* [1985] 2 All ER 1077.

---

## 4.6 Interim binding procedure

Section 108(3) of the Act requires the contract to provide that the decision of the adjudicator is binding until the dispute is finally determined by legal proceedings (in court or arbitration) or by agreement. The parties may, pursuant to s 108(3), agree to accept the decision of the adjudicator as finally determining the dispute. The adjudicator's award will only be as good as the parties' willingness to honour or the courts' willingness to enforce it. Enforcement is addressed in Chapter 7. The effect of the adjudicator's award is considered *below*.

### 4.6.1 No power to alter substantive rights

It is implicit in s 108(2)(*f*) that the adjudicator must, in reaching his decision, apply the law of the contract to the facts of the dispute as found by him. He has no power to alter the parties' substantive rights—his role is to ascertain them. The contractual obligation to comply with the award until it is overturned may be in conflict with another right under the contract. For example, an adjudicator may find that one party is not entitled to assign the contract in circumstances where the contract gives him a right to do so. The contractual right to rely upon the award may be in conflict with another obligation under the contract. For example, an architect may, in reliance upon an adjudicator's award refuse to assign copyright in drawings in circumstances where he has a contractual obligation under his contract so to do. If the adjucator's ascertainment of the parties substantive rights is wrong, the parties can have his decision overturned in court or arbitration.

### 4.6.2 Consequences of reversing award

That the award may be overturned in arbitration or court proceedings implies that if it is, a benefit obtained from an award which is overturned must be disgorged. So, money paid over should be repaid. However, if the adjudicator has made a non-money award it may not be possible to reverse the consequences of compliance with or reliance on it. Actions cannot be undone. It is unlikely that the legislature intended that the parties' rights pursuant to the construction contract should be changed even on an interim basis by the adjudicator's award. If this is correct, when the award is overturned the conduct of the parties is judged in accordance with rights as ultimately established and not as found by the adjudicator.

Thus, if an adjudicator decides that a sub-contractor is entitled to suspend performance of his work for non-payment, in accordance with s 112 of the Act, a sub-contractor suspends work in reliance upon that decision at his own risk. If the adjudicator's award is subsequently overturned in court or arbitration, the sub-contractor will wrongfully have suspended and will be liable for any delay or disruption caused. If the adjudicator confirms the design of an engineer, and the engineer, therefore, incorporates it into his work, he may nevertheless be in breach of his contract if the design is negligent or non-compliant with the contract. If this analysis is correct, the effect of the adjudicator's award is to make an interim regulation of the parties' rights (in accordance with their contractual entitlements as best ascertainable within the time available) without prejudice to the parties actual rights as ultimately established.[41]

### 4.6.3 Third parties

As with any other contractual right, the adjudicator's award does not bind third parties. So, if an adjudicator confirms a sub-contractor's design which is incorporated into the work, the main contractor is not excused from liability to the employer for breach of contract if that design is in fact defective or non-compliant with the contract. If the adjudicator finds that an engineer's design is adequate, the engineer will not be entitled to rely upon the award if the design is in fact defective and causes damage or injury to a third party. The adjudicator's award may be relevant to the issue of negligence but will not excuse the engineer if, notwithstanding the award, his design is negligent. If it is the employer who suffers loss in consequence of the negligent design, he may recover from the engineer by overturning the adjudicator's award.

---

41 See para 7.6.

---

# 5

# Additional Contractual
# Requirements

## 5.1 Introduction

### 5.1.1 Skeletal requirements of s 108

It is assumed in this chapter that the parties wish to avoid the Scheme. If they do not, they need make no provision for adjudication. Otherwise, their contract must comply with s 108. It is not open to the parties to make provision complying with s 108 in part, leaving the Scheme to apply in part. The contract must comply with s 108 in its entirety or the adjudication provisions of the Scheme will apply in their entirety. If the parties wish to incorporate some only of the provisions of the Scheme, they may do so expressly in a contract which complies with s 108. The requirements of s 108 are few and are discussed in Chapters 3 and 4. To the extent that the Act makes no requirement, the parties may draft their adjudication agreement as they see fit. This chapter discusses a number of issues which are not addressed by the Act and which the parties should make provision for in their contract. It is within the power of the parties to make provision to maximise the effect of adjudication. It is also within their power to make provision to restrict the effect of adjudication to that strictly required by s 108.

### 5.1.2 Standard forms

There is no one correct set of adjudication provisions. The terms suitable for any particular contract will depend upon what the parties wish to achieve. Many institutions will publish standard form adjudication provisions intended to comply with s 108.[1] As with any other standard form provisions, these may represent a specific industry interest or a compromise between differing industry interests. They may not represent in any particular case the perspective and intentions of the parties to the contract. However, standard form adjudication provisions will often be acceptable to the parties as published or with minor amendments. It is hoped that this book will be of assistance not only in the drafting of adjudication provisions but also in the consideration and amendment of the terms of standard form adjudication rules which the parties may wish to adopt.

### 5.1.3   Two contracts

Any adjudication conducted pursuant to s 108 should involve two contracts. One is the construction contract between the parties which is required to comply with s 108(1)–(4). The other is the contract between the parties and the adjudicator. Section 108 does not address this contract at all. Section 108(2) appears to assume that the construction contract may impose obligations upon the adjudicator.[2] This is clearly not the case unless the adjudicator is party to the construction contract which will be rare. The 'contract' referred to in s 108(2) must mean the construction contract between the parties and not the contract with the adjudicator.[3] It is therefore, possible that the construction contract complies with s 108, but that the adjudicator's terms of appointment do not reflect the construction contract in relevant respects. While the adjudicator's authority will ordinarily be construed so as to reflect relevant provisions from the construction contract there may be circumstances in which such construction is not possible. It is therefore desirable for the parties to regulate their relationship with the adjudicator by express contract.

---

1   Many of the standard forms had not published their amendments at the time of going to press
2   For example, s 108(2)(e) requires the 'contract' to impose a duty of impartiality upon the adjudicator.
3   Nowhere is the contract with the adjudicator referred to in s 108. The 'contract' in s 108(2) clearly refers back to the 'contract' in s 108(1) which is the construction contract.

---

## 5.2   The adjudicator

### 5.2.1   Contractual relationship with parties

The adjudicator's relationship with the parties should be governed by contract.[4] The adjudicator's rights against and duties towards the parties will be contractual if the parties expressly agree his terms of appointment or if by their conduct, for example by participation in the adjudication, they are deemed to accept terms proffered by the adjudicator or implied as a matter of law. However, if, upon proper analysis, a contract cannot be spelt out of the adjudicator's relationship with the parties or one of them, the relationship will be governed by the general law. In this case an adjudicator may have only a restitutionary claim for remuneration[5] and may depend for immunity from suit upon successfully drawing an analogy with the arbitrator's immunity at common law.[6] The adjudicator does not have the statutory rights, powers and protection afforded to arbitrators by the Arbitration Act 1996,[7] nor is there any established body of law setting out the rights, duties and obligations of adjudicators at common law. In the absence of contractual provision the adjudicator's position is unclear and must be analysed from the general law. An adjudicator should regard it as fundamentally important that a contract is in place between him and the parties or at least one of them.[8] It is assumed in this chapter that this is the case.

### 5.2.2 Qualifications

The Act imposes no requirements in terms of the number, identity, qualifications or expertise of individuals, firms or companies who may be appointed to act as adjudicators. It is not necessary for an adjudicator to be 'qualified' as such nor accredited and entered upon the list of a nominating institution. In practise, it is likely that adjudicators who are named in the contract will be chosen for their expertise and those nominated by an institution will qualify for nomination only by reason of their expertise. It must, however, remain a risk that if the construction industry makes frequent recourse to adjudication, the demand for adjudicators will exceed supply with a consequent increase in the fees charged by adjudicators and/or an influx of adjudicators inadequately equipped to fulfil the role with the inevitable reduction in quality. Parties who require an adjudicator of a particular professional discipline or with particular experience[9] or expertise should make this requirement expressly by their contract and, if appropriate, choose a nominating institution accordingly.

There is no reason why a contract should not require the appointment of a panel of adjudicators. The contract may, alternatively or in addition, make provision for an adjudicator to keep himself informed of events on site at all times and maintain a continued involvement throughout the project. Such an arrangement would usually require the adjudicator to be paid a regular retainer in recognition of the fact that if he is to be available at all times his ability to undertake other commitments will be limited. The expense of such a provision may be justified on substantial projects. There is no reason why the adjudicator should not be a company or partnership. Partnerships of accountants are often appointed experts to value shares in companies. Multi-disciplinary practices will often be able to provide the expertise to resolve a dispute whatever its nature.

### 5.2.3 Duties of the adjudicator

The powers and duties of the adjudicator derive from the contract conferring jurisdiction upon him. The parties to that contract may confer such power upon the adjudicator as they see fit, for example the power (and duty) to review certificates, act as *aimable compositeur* or make an interim decision on the basis of some agreed formulation between the parties, such as the balance of convenience. In the absence of provision to the contrary, it will be the duty of the adjudicator to resolve the dispute by ascertaining the parties' legal entitlements which he must do by applying the law of the contract to the facts of the dispute as found by him. His decision must be reached within 28 days (s 108(2)(*c*)). The contract must require the adjudicator to act impartially (s 108(2)(*e*)). The adjudicator's terms of appointment should make provision accordingly. They should also make provision for any other duty which the parties wish to impose upon the adjudicator.[10]

### 5.2.4 Level of adjudicator's fees

The vast majority of adjudicators will expect remuneration for their services. If not expressly agreed, the right to and the level of remuneration and the time by which it is to be paid will be implied as a matter of law. The law will imply an obligation upon the parties to pay the adjudicator a reasonable sum within a reasonable time. What is reasonable will take into account factors such as the time spent by the adjudicator on the dispute, the nature and complexity of the dispute, the level of skill and experience required to resolve it, current commercial rates and possibly also the value of the claims adjudicated. It is undesirable from the adjudicator's point of view that his terms of remuneration should be left to be implied by law. The uncertain extent of what is reasonable may be manipulated by disappointed or unscrupulous parties to their advantage.

### 5.2.5 Ascertaining adjudicator's fees

There is no procedure for taxing an adjudicator's costs such as exists for parties dissatisfied with the level of an arbitrator's remuneration.[11] Challenge by the parties to the level of the adjudicator's fees or substantiation by the adjudicator of those fees may require court proceedings for resolution. If the adjudicator is unwilling to release his award pending payment of his fees, dispute as to the level of those fees may cause the parties significant inconvenience. To reduce the risk to both the adjudicator and the parties, the adjudicator should obtain the agreement of the parties or one of them, preferably in writing, to his terms of remuneration. However, the above risks cannot be eliminated altogether. Agreement to payment of the adjudicator's hourly rate does not imply any acceptance of the number of hours necessary for the adjudicator to spend upon the reference. The number of hours spent and charged by the adjudicator may come as an unpleasant surprise to the parties and is equally capable of giving rise to intractable disputes as to the adjudicator's remuneration entitlement as disagreement over rates. There is little that can be done about this save impose a limit upon the adjudicator's remuneration, which step requires the consent of both parties and the adjucator.

### 5.2.6 Liability for fees as between parties

The construction contract should make provision for liability of the parties to pay the adjudicator's fees. That provision might be that the claimant is to pay those fees in the first instance subject to a right to recover all or part of them if successful in the adjudication. Or, the contract might provide that the parties are to bear an equal proportion of the adjudicator's fees either with or without a right of recovery following the outcome of the adjudication. The contract may also provide that in the event that one party does not pay his share of the adjudicator's fees, the other may pay them and recover them, if appropriate, from the defaulting party as a debt.[12]

### 5.2.7 Liability for fees as against the adjudicator

By analogy with liability for an arbitrator's fees the parties will be jointly liable for the adjudicator's fees.[13] It is not clear, in the context of arbitration, whether liability for the arbitrator's fees is, in addition to being joint, several also.[14] It is within the power of the adjudicator and the parties to put the issue beyond doubt.

The adjudicator's terms of appointment should specify whether the parties are to bear joint and several liability for payment of his fees or joint liability only. Such provision should be made whether or not the adjudicator has power to order costs (including his fees) to be paid by one party only. If the defendant refuses to give a satisfactory undertaking to the adjudicator in respect of his fees, the adjudicator should ensure that he is able to recover the entire amount of his fees from the claimant.

### 5.2.8  Expenses

The adjudicator's terms of appointment should make express provision for reimbursement of expenses additional to his fee. They should specify the disbursements or expenses to be charged extra, for example, room hire, transcript charges, copying, fax charges, travel and subsistence. Unless the adjudicator has express or implied authority from the parties to appoint legal or technical advisors, and recover from them the costs of so doing, he will be unable to recover from the parties any fees payable to such legal or technical advisors.[15] His terms of appointment should, where appropriate, expressly entitle him to recover such fees as a disbursement.

### 5.2.9  Fees—excess of jurisdiction

Notwithstanding best efforts and skill, the adjudicator may be found to have acted in excess of jurisdiction. In this event, he may be entitled to no remuneration. His entitlement to fees cannot derive from an invalid award (*Darlington BC v Waring & Gillow (Holdings) Ltd* [1988] EGLR 159). Whether he is entitled to remuneration in whole or in part and from whom will depend upon the precise circumstances of the case. A defendant who objects to the adjudicator taking jurisdiction over the dispute and who takes no part in the proceedings can rarely be subject to an implied contract to pay the adjudicator's fees. On the other hand, a claimant who persists in the adjudication notwithstanding the defendant's objections may, without great difficulty, be found to have impliedly agreed to pay the adjudicator's fees notwithstanding that the objection to jurisdiction may be well-founded. An objection to jurisdiction taken only after the adjudicator's award may not justify the parties or one of them in refusing to pay the adjudicator's fees—the parties may be found to have acquiesced in the adjudication. A wise adjudicator will make express provision in his terms of appointment to ensure that, notwithstanding excess of jurisdiction, and notwithstanding that his award may subsequently be overturned, the parties (or at least the claimant) are liable to pay his fees.

### 5.2.10  Securing payment

The adjudicator's terms of appointment should make express provision for securing payment of his fees. Payment in advance or on account is the most effective security. If the adjudicator is not willing or able to insist upon payment in advance or on account, he should ensure that he has the right, pursuant to his terms of appointment, to exercise a lien upon his award for payment of his fees and expenses.[16] A lien on his award will often be less effective as a means of securing payment than requiring payment in advance. This is because if neither party is sufficiently anxious to obtain the award, neither may pay the adjudicator's fees in order to lift the lien. This will be a particular risk in circumstances where it becomes clear during the course of the adjudication that the claimant will be unsuccessful. He will have no interest in paying the adjudicator's fees to lift the lien and the defendant will not need to do so—he is not at risk until an adverse adjudicator's award has been issued against him. If the adjudicator's fees are not secured, his right of recovery will be by action in the courts.

---

4   The relationship between the parties and an arbitrator is usually analysed as a contractual one See, however, Mustill and Boyd, *Commercial Arbitration*, p 220.
5   There may be circumstances in which a restitutionary claim to payment will be entirely inadequate. This may be the case where, for example, the parties compromise the dispute before award is delivered or if the adjudicator, through no fault of his own exceeds his jurisdiction and his award is a nullity.
6   See para **4.5.4**.
7   See, for example, s 29 of the Arbitration Act 1996 which gives arbitrations statutory immunity from suit.
8   See para **4.2.9**.
9   There is no reason why a person engaged in a professional capacity in relation to the project such as architect or engineer, should not be appointed adjudicator. This will often be an unattractive option for at least one of the parties.
10  Section 33 of the Arbitration Act provides a useful, if general, formula which, with minor adaptations, may be appropriate for adjudication: 'The tribunal shall—(a) act fairly and impartially, as between the parties, giving each party a reasonable opportunity of putting his case and dealing with that of his opponent, and (b) adopt procedures suitable to the circumstances of the particular case, avoiding unnecessary delay or expense, so as to provide a fair means for the resolution of the matters falling to be determined'.
11  Arbitration Act 1996, s 28(2).
12  The entitlement to recover these fees probably follows upon proper contractual analysis even without express provision.
13  Assuming that the defendant can be fixed with contractual liability, express or implied. See discussion at paras **4.2.9** and **5.2.1**; see also *Crampton and Holt v Ridley & Co* (1887) 20 QBD 48.
14  See Mustill and Boyd, *Commercial Arbitration*, p 235, n13.
15  There is no equivalent in the context of adjudication of s 27 of the Arbitration Act.
16  He may, by analogy with an arbitrator's rights, have a lien pursuant to the common law. It is preferable that the issue is put beyond doubt by contract. The exercise of a lien on his fees is probably not inconsistent with the adjudicator's obligation to reach his decision within 28 days. This is not an obligation to deliver to the parties his award within 28 days

---

## 5.3   Procedure

### 5.3.1   Required by the Act

The few procedural requirements of the Act are dealt with in Chapter 4.

### 5.3.2   Not required by the Act

The Act gives no guidance beyond s 108 on procedures to be followed before the adjudicator is to reach his decision. The parties are free to agree the procedure they wish to follow. Alternatively, they may leave all or only some issues of procedure to be fixed by the adjudicator. In the very limited time available for the conduct of the adjudication proceedings, it may not be possible to replicate the sort of procedures familiar in court and arbitration proceedings. It will often be undesirable to attempt to do so. Extensive disclosure of documents may do little more than confuse issues. Oral hearings may be unnecessary and overburden parties anxious to avoid the expense of lawyers.[17] On the other hand, if the dispute involves contested issues of fact, an oral hearing with witnesses and cross-examination may be the most reliable way to assess disputed fact. The parties may prefer the formality of an oral hearing to bring them together, thus facilitating settlement. The appropriate procedure for the resolution of disputes will usually depend upon the nature of the dispute and prevailing circumstances.[18] In the absence of agreement between the parties as to procedure, the adjudicator will be master of his own procedure and have power to organise the proceedings as he sees fit.[19]

### 5.3.3   Procedural requirements by contract

If the contract specifies procedural steps to be followed, it must ensure that they are scheduled in such a way as to allow the adjudicator time to take the initiative in ascertaining fact and law[20] and consider his award within the period prescribed by s 108(2)(c). The parties are free to agree matters such as whether there is to be an oral hearing or only written submissions,[21] representation and attendance at hearings, the timing and length of submissions, power to amend submissions and any other procedural matter which they consider important. The power of the adjudicator to take the initiative in ascertaining fact or law does not of itself prescribe any particular procedure but it may justify failure of the adjudicator to follow certain procedures considered obligatory in adversarial proceedings.[22] There is no merit in considering in this book all potentially applicable procedural steps. What is appropriate in any particular case will depend upon the nature of the dispute and the wishes of the parties. For this reason it will often be desirable to leave procedure to be agreed between the parties after the dispute has arisen and, failing agreement, to the discretion of the adjudicator.[23]

### 5.3.4   Laws of evidence

The obligation to apply all the laws of evidence probably arises only in proceedings of a judicial rather than administrative or inquisitorial nature. However, there are degrees of judicial hearings (*Re Commission for Racial Equality* [1980] 3 All ER 265) and the closer a procedure approximates to a purely administrative or inquisitorial one the more relaxed an approach can be expected to the rules of evidence.[24] In each case it will be necessary to examine the nature of the inquiry in which the issue arises, which in turn requires consideration of the powers under which the tribunal is operating (*R v Deputy Industrial Injuries Commissioner ex p Moore* [1965] 1 QB 456). Whether an adjudicator is conducting proceedings of a sufficiently judicial nature to justify the applicability of certain, and if so what, rules of evidence depends upon the terms of the adjudication agreement between the parties from which the adjudicator derives jurisdiction and which define the nature of the adjudicator's role.[25] Certain rules of evidence may be justified on public policy grounds or on grounds of fairness.[26]

It may be suggested that the adjudicator's power to take the initiative in ascertaining fact and law dictates that his procedure is an inquisitorial one in which the laws of evidence are inapplicable. So stated, this view is oversimplified. To the extent that the adjudicator himself ascertains fact, for example, when conducting exercises analogous to those performed by a valuer,[27] the rules of evidence can clearly have little role. However, when hearing and assessing the rival contentions of the parties, there is no particular reason why the rationale of any particular rule of evidence should not be as applicable in the context of adjudication as in arbitration. The Arbitration Act 1996[28] envisages the arbitrator's power to take the initiative in ascertaining fact and law co-existing comfortably with application of the laws of evidence. It is suggested that it is open to the parties to require the adjudicator to take into account only that evidence which would be admissible in a court of law or to give it the weight that would be attached to it in court proceedings.[29] In practice, this will be difficult to police and there will be no effective sanction for failure to comply. However, it is not inconsistent with the adjudicator's power to take the initiative in ascertaining fact or law. It simply requires him to do so only by use of legally admissible evidence.

---

17  The burden of advocacy, even in informal proceedings, is a heavy one for a layman.
18  Section 34 of the Arbitration Act 1996 leaves decisions on procedural and evidential matters to the arbitrator, subject to the right of the parties to agree any matter.
19  By analogy with arbitration. See *Bremer Vulkan v South India Shipping Co* [1981] AC 909 at p 985. See also *Carlisle Place Investments v Wimpey* 15 BLR 108 at p 116.
20  Section 108(2)(*f*).
21  Subject to the adjudicator's power to take the initiative in ascertaining fact and law. See *Town & Country Properties v Wiltshier* 44 BLR 109, where an arbitrator was removed for misconduct for disallowing an oral hearing. He was criticised for conducting inquisitorial proceedings.
22  See paras **4.4.1–4.4.2**.
23  See s 34 of the Arbitration Act 1996.
24  Exclusionary rules of evidence in civil proceedings are few.
25  See para **4.5.4**.
26  For example, legal professional privilege.
27  Such as inspecting alleged defects and forming a professional opinion thereon.
28  Section 34(2)(*f*) and (*g*).
29  See s 34(2)(*f*) of the Arbitration Act 1996.

---

## 5.4   Powers of the adjudicator

### 5.4.1   Interlocutory powers

In the absence of power conferred by contract, the adjudicator has no jurisdiction to make interlocutory orders such as for the preservation of property or evidence or the provision of security for costs.[30] However, the contract must enable the adjudicator to take the initiative in ascertaining fact and law,[31] which implies interlocutory powers, such as the power to order disclosure of documents or examination of property or witnesses relevant to the dispute. Where the order which the adjudicator seeks to make is justified by the adjudicator's power to take the initiative and reach a decision, it will be within his jurisdiction. Where it is made in order to preserve evidence for later court or arbitration proceedings or to regulate the interlocutory positions of the parties, for example in relation to costs, it will be beyond his jurisdiction unless within specific power granted by the contract. The adjudicator has no power to compel compliance with any order he may make. He cannot commit for contempt. He has no power to administer oaths[32] or compel the attendance of witnesses. It is unlikely that a *subpoena* may issue from the High Court to compel the attendance of a witness at adjudication proceedings (*Currie v Chief Constable of Surrey* (1982) 1 WLR 215). Nor does he have power to make peremptory orders and enforce them by sanction.

The circumstances of an adjudication will often make interlocutory orders inappropriate even if the adjudicator is given jurisdiction to make them. For example, in circumstances where the adjudicator must reach his decision within 28 days it is entirely inappropriate for him to stay the proceedings pending the provision of security for costs. The adjudicator should be slow to draw adverse inferences against a party who fails to comply with his orders. The timetable and circumstances of an adjudication procedure may cause serious practical difficulties[33] for even the best intentioned party.

### 5.4.2 Power to award interest

There is no common law right to interest for the late payment of money nor is interest available as general damages for breach (*President of India v La Pintada Navogacion Co SA, La Pintada* [1984] 2 Lloyd's Rep 9).[34] Interest may be awarded only pursuant to statute or contract or as special damages for breach of contract (see, for example, *Holbeach Plant Hire Ltd v Anglian Water Authority* 14 Con LR 101). There is no statute which entitles an adjudicator to award interest. In the absence of a contractually conferred power, the adjudicator has no jurisdiction so to do. In this case a claimant seeking the recovery of interest must overcome the hurdle of proving special damages for breach. The contract should provide whether the adjudicator may award interest on any sum found to be due. It should also provide details of the interest that may be awarded such as rate, compounding details if appropriate, period of interest, etc. Alternatively, the contract may leave these details to the discretion of the adjudicator. Whether interest is to be recoverable is a commercial decision for the parties.

### 5.4.3 Power to award costs

In the absence of power conferred either by contract or by statute, the adjudicator has no jurisdiction to order one party to pay the costs expended by another in the adjudication proceedings. Power to award costs is conferred upon courts and arbitrators expressly by statute.[35] There is no statute which confers such power upon adjudicators. If the parties wish the adjudicator to have power to award costs, they must confer such power upon him. Conferring the power to make a costs order may deter frivolous applications for adjudication. Not conferring the power to make a costs order may encourage late payment for which there may be little effective sanction. The parties must decide the provision as regards costs best likely to promote their commercial interests.

### 5.4.4   Level of costs

The contract should specify the basis upon which the adjudicator may award costs and in particular whether he must act judicially[36] in so doing. It should also specify the level of costs that may be awarded, for example, whether costs are to be awarded on indemnity terms or on some other and if so what basis. In the absence of provision to the contrary, the level of costs recoverable will not automatically be subject to the deductions habitually made in High Court and other taxations but will depend upon the construction of the contractual provision by which the entitlement to costs arises. So, a bare obligation upon one party to pay costs expended by another does not imply recovery of costs calculated on the party and party basis.[37] It may, however, imply an obligation to pay only such costs as were directly incurred in connection with the adjudication, thereby excluding, for example, the costs incurred in dealings with insurers. It may also exclude costs unreasonably incurred such as for example the costs of employing a second expert for a 'second opinion'.

### 5.4.5   Assessing costs

There is no procedure for the taxation of costs incurred during adjudication proceedings. There is no right of access to the High Court taxation procedures such as is available for the taxation of arbitration costs awards.[38] Provision should be made in the contract for the ascertainment of the costs recoverable pursuant to an adjudicator's costs award. Such provision might be that the adjudicator may tax costs in his award.[39] Alternatively, the parties may agree that a particular firm of costs draftsmen or a firm nominated by the adjudicator should carry out the taxation. In this case the decision of the draftsman should be required to be final and binding to avoid further disputes.[40] If no provision is made for the ascertainment of recoverable costs, payment of the costs order will be no more than a contractual obligation the quantum of which is ascertainable only by further adjudication, arbitration or court action.

### 5.4.6   Other powers

The parties may confer such power as they consider appropriate upon the adjudicator. For example, they may confer power to open up, review and revise certificates issued under the contract,[41] they may confer power to act as aimable compositeur[42] or make a decision on some basis other than the parties' contractual entitlements.[43] The contract may even leave the adjudicator to complete details of the parties' obligations left unclarified in the construction contract. In *F&G Sykes (Wessex) Ltd v Fine Fare Ltd* [1967] 1 Lloyd's Rep 53, an arbitrator was found on the wording of the particular clause under consideration to have power to determine the number of chicks that would be reasonable for the vendor to sell to the purchaser in a particular year. There is no reason why similar power should not be conferred upon an adjudicator. If the adjudicator is to have power beyond determining the parties' substantive rights in accordance with the law, equivalent power should be conferred upon the tribunal to which the dispute is to be referred for final resolution. In the absence of such power the adjudicator's award may be, *de facto*, final and irreversible in default of a tribunal with power to review it. If the adjudicator is to have power which a court does not have, the procedures available for overturning the adjudicator's award may be restricted to arbitration. This is because it is not always possible to confer upon a court jurisdiction which it does not have but which it would need to review the adjudicator's decision.[44]

---

30  Such powers are conferred on courts and arbitrators by statute. None is applicable to adjudication.
31  Section 108(2)(*f*).
32  See *Halsbury's Laws*, Vol 17, para 319.
33  The statutory timetable makes no allowance for the possibility of personnel with relevant knowledge being unavailable through illness, holidays, having left the employ of a party nor the inherent delays in retrieving archived documents.
34  See also *President of India v Lips Maritime Corporation, The Lips* [1987] 2 Lloyd's Rep 311.
35  See, for example, s 51 of the Supreme Court Act 1981 and s 61 of the Arbitration Act 1996.
36  Section 61(2) of the Arbitration Act provides that unless the parties otherwise agree, an arbitrator awarding costs should proceed on the general principle that costs should follow the event unless this is not appropriate to the whole or part of the costs.
37  The taxed down costs awarded in High Court taxations.
38  See s 63(4) of the Arbitration Act 1996.
39  Arbitrator's have this power. See s 63(3) of the Arbitration Act 1996.
40  This procedure will be equivalent to an expert determination.
41  See para **3.4.6–3.4.9**.
42  See para **4.2.17**.
43  See para **4.2.17**.
44  See the argument in *Tarmac Construction Ltd v Esso Petroleum Co Ltd* (1996) 51 Con LR 187, which failed on the wording of the contract in that particular case but which might well succeed in other contexts.

---

## 5.5    The award

### 5.5.1    Form

The contract must require the adjudicator to reach his decision within 28 days of referral of the dispute.[45] The Act makes no further requirements in relation to the adjudicator's decision. The parties may require it to be in a particular form, for example in writing, signed and dated or alternatively, they may specify that it be given orally. If it is to be given in writing, they may require that it be served in a particular way, for example by fax.

### 5.5.2    Reasons

The contract may require that the decision be given either with or without reasons. There is no statutory requirement in this regard. An award without reasons is more difficult to challenge than one for which reasons are provided.[46] It will be difficult to know from an award without reasons what matters have been decided in the award.[47] Reasons may enable a party who has erred in the performance of his contractual obligations to amend his conduct for the future. The obligation to give reasons may provide an incentive to the adjudicator to formulate and express his decision with greater care. Reasons may enable a party to assess whether to proceed further with the dispute and seek to overturn the adjudicator's award or accept his decision as final. Ultimately, whether the parties wish the adjudicator to provide reasons for his decision will depend upon commercial considerations including the nature and quantum of the award and the parties' attitudes to the bindingness of the award when published. The contract and the adjudicator's terms of appointment should make express provision for a reasoned award if this is what the parties wish. In the absence of express provision, the right to reasons will depend upon implication. A simple obligation upon the adjudicator to reach a decision may not be sufficient to give rise to an implied obligation to provide reasons for that decision.

### 5.5.3 Formal requirements of award

There are no formal requirements of the award except as may be agreed between the parties. Arbitration awards must satisfy certain substantive criteria for their validity.[48] It is unlikely that the law which has developed in the context of arbitration will be slavishly followed in the context of adjudication. Greater latitude can be expected of a process which is intended to be speedy, approximate and interim. However, the criteria applicable to arbitration awards may be such that if they are not satisfied, a court cannot sensibly enforce the award. So, an arbitration award must be cogent, complete, certain and final.[49] A court may be unable to enforce an adjudicator's award which does not satisfy these criteria. It is suggested that in any particular case, a court will look not for the satisfaction of formal rules but at the simple question whether the award can properly be enforced.

### 5.5.4 *Functus officio*

Once the adjudicator has made his award he will be *functus officio*. This means that the adjudicator's function is discharged. He cannot revisit his award and make changes to it either for the purpose of correcting an error, whether substantive or merely clerical or for taking into account fact or law which was not previously available to him. There will be no means by which a merely clerical slip may be corrected (*Gosden v Funnell* (1889) 15 TLR 547)—there is no equivalent in the context of adjudication of s 57 of the Arbitration Act 1996. *Functus officio* is not a concept restricted to courts (*Re VGM Holdings Ltd* [1941] 3 All ER 417) or arbitrators (*Mordue v Palmer* (1870) 6 Ch App 22), but applies also to administrative tribunals (see, for example, *Heron Corporation Ltd v Manchester CC* (1977) 33 P&CR 268; *Preston BC v Secretary of State for the Environment* [1978] JPL 548). There is no reason why it should not apply also to adjudicators—the rationale applies with equal if not greater force to a procedure which is required to be complete within 28 days. The parties may not be free to agree in the construction contract that the adjudicator may correct a slip—the result of such agreement could be that the award as corrected is not reached within the 28-day period prescribed by s 108(2)(*c*).

45 Section 108(2)(*c*).
46 See Chapter 7. See also *Healds Foods Ltd v Hyde Dairies Ltd* (1994) unreported, 12 December.
47 For the significance of this, see para **7.1.2**.
48 See Mustill & Boyd, *Commercial Arbitration*, p 382.
49 See Mustill & Boyd, *Commercial Arbitration*, pp 384–7.

## 5.6 Confidentiality

### 5.6.1 Implied duty of confidentiality

The Act makes no provision dealing with the question whether adjudication is a private procedure. The common law can offer no precedent. Arbitration is a private procedure (*The Eastern Saga* [1984] 2 Lloyd's Rep 373; *Hassneh Insurance Co of Israel v Stuart J Mewin* [1993] 2 Lloyd's Rep 243; *Esso Australia Resources Ltd v Plowman* [1994] 1 VR 1), but it does not follow by analogy that adjudication is. The implied term of privacy in arbitration is justified by 'a practice which has been universal in London for hundreds of years' (*Hassneh Insurance Co of Israel v Stuart J Mewin* [1993] 2 Lloyd's Rep 243). Adjudication is a relatively novel procedure and has not developed a practice in this regard. Parties to arbitration agreements may choose arbitration for the resolution of their dispute in order to preserve privacy. Parties to adjudication under the Act do not necessarily choose adjudication at all. In the absence of authority on this issue, the parties should make confidentiality an express obligation if they wish to preserve privacy.

### 5.6.2 Limits of duty

A duty of 'confidentiality' of itself has no defined limits. The contract should specify what the duty of confidentiality entails. The duty of confidentiality arising from implied terms of an arbitration agreement excludes from the hearing strangers to the dispute.[50] It prevents the disclosure to third parties of documents created for the purpose of the arbitration and evidence as to what was said or done during the course of the arbitration. An express duty of confidentiality in an adjudication agreement should provide likewise. There are limits to the duty of confidentiality in arbitration agreements such as where disclosure is necessary in the course of application to court in connection with the arbitration[51] or where disclosure is reasonably necessary for the protection of a party's interests (*Hassneh Insurance Co of Israel v Stuart J Mewin* [1993] 2 Lloyd's Rep 243; *Insurance Co v Lloyds Syndicate* [1995] 1 Lloyd's Rep 272; see also the discussion of Brooking J in *Esso Australia Resources Ltd v Plowman* [1994] 1 VR 1). A contractual duty of confidentiality will not excuse a party from its duty of disclosure of documents in subsequent court or arbitration proceedings (*Dolling-Baker v Merrett* [1990] 1 WLR 1205; *Science Research Council v Nasse* [1980] AC 1028), nor will it defeat a *subpoena* (*London & Leeds Estates Ltd v Paribas Ltd (No 2)* [1995] 2 EG 134). The existence of the duty of confidentiality will, however, be a relevant factor for the court to consider in the exercise of its discretion and in deciding whether disclosure of the documents in question is necessary for fairly disposing of the case or whether there are 'possibly less costly ways of obtaining the information which is sought which do not involve any breach of the implied undertaking' (*Dolling Baker v Merrett* [1990] 1 WLR 1205).

### 5.6.3  Privilege

Legal professional privilege should be honoured in adjucation as in court or arbitration proceedings. Adjudication proceedings will not normally attract 'without prejudice' privilege. This is because it will not usually be possible to justify privilege on the basis that the adjudication proceedings were conducted as a 'without prejudice' attempt to compromise a dispute. The procedure is one forced upon the defendant by s108 and has as its object the making of an interim enforceable decision which the parties do not accept as finally resolving the dispute. Adjudication is not about facilitating compromise. Adjudication proceedings will probably not attract 'litigation' privilege either. In the absence of privilege documents such as inter party correspondence, draft experts reports and the reports of experts not in fact called in the adjudication proceedings may be put in evidence or compelled to be disclosed in subsequent proceedings. Contractually agreed confidentiality, even subject to restrictions imposed by law, will be the most effective means of reducing this risk.

### 5.6.4  Adjudicator as witness

It is common in expert determination and voluntary adjudication agreements for the parties to provide that the expert/adjudicator should not be called as a witness in subsequent court or arbitration proceedings to give evidence about what occurred in the expert determination or adjudication procedure. Often it will be unnecessary to call the adjudicator to give such evidence. There will usually be other witnesses available to give evidence as to what was said or done during the proceedings if such evidence is relevant. In many other cases the evidence which the adjudicator could give will not be legally relevant. For instance, it will not often be relevant to hear how or why an adjudicator reached the decision he did reach. In some cases, however, such evidence may be relevant.

A provision restricting the calling of the adjudicator as a witness will be effective and enforceable if relied upon to aid an essential characteristic of the procedure, for example its finality.[52] There is no reason why such a clause should not be effective unless shown to be contrary to public policy. It may be ineffective as contrary to public policy if its effect is to prevent the courts exercising their statutory function (*E Rotheray & Sons Ltd v Carlo Bedarido & Co* [1961] 1 Lloyd's Rep 220) or if used in an attempt to perpetrate a fraud. In any particular case, the effect of the clause and its context must be considered before any conclusion may be drawn as to the extent of its enforceability. In the absence of such a clause, the adjudicator will be a competent and compellable witness to give whatever relevant evidence he can.

50  *The Eastern Saga* [1984] 2 Lloyd's Rep 373.
51  For example, appeals or applications to have the arbitrator removed.
52  *Healds Foods Ltd v Hyde Dairies Ltd* (1994) unreported, 12 December. Adjudication proceedings under the Act will often not be final.

## 5.7  Multi-party adjudication

### 5.7.1  Desirability

As the name suggests, multi-party adjudication involves adjudication between more than two parties. Such a procedure may involve little more than a simple dispute the result of which determines the rights of more than two parties. For example, a question of defective works may dictate rights and obligations as between employer and main contractor and between main contractor and subcontractor. Alternatively, multi-party adjudication may give rise to a proliferation of issues with claims and cross-claims between the various parties. The rationale of the right to adjudication as envisaged by the Act was to create a simple, cheap and quick procedure for the resolution of disputes. Multi-party adjudication will often thwart this objective.

### 5.7.2  Time limits

The structure and detail of the Act does not lend itself to multi-party adjudication. The time within which the adjudicator must reach his decision will usually render multi party adjudication inappropriate. If all parties agree to submit to multi-party adjudication and to extend the time for the procedure accordingly,[53] it is certainly possible. Multi-party adjudication is possible only by agreement of all the parties[54] and whilst contracts may provide a mechanism by which adjudications can be consolidated, such provision will rarely be effective. It is very difficult to make provision in the construction contract for multi-party adjudication without infringing the terms of s 108. This is because a party cannot be required to advance his claim in adjudication to dovetail with any other claim. He has, pursuant to s 108(2)(*a*), the right to serve notice of adjudication 'at any time' and the statutory time periods run from the date of this notice.

### 5.7.3  Power of attorney

It is not open to the parties to extend the time set out in s 108 in advance of referral of the dispute. It is therefore not possible in the construction contract to make provision extending the time within which adjudication must be carried out with a view to facilitating multi-party adjudication. It may be possible, by use of a power of attorney, for the donor of the power to confer authority upon the donee exercisable after referral of a dispute, to agree on behalf of the donor to extend time in the adjudication in order to facilitate multi-party adjudication. In many contracts the complexity of such provision will be unwelcome. Many parties will be unwilling to accept the relinquishment of control that a power of attorney entails. Nor is it certain that such power of attorney will be effective. It may infringe s 108 as constituting in effect an extension of time agreed prior to referral of the dispute to adjudication.[55]

### 5.7.4   Substantive obligations to bind third parties

The contract may provide, as a substantive obligation, that if an adjudication award is made which relates to the performance of a person not party to the proceedings, he will be bound by that award as if it had been made in proceedings to which he was a party. So, if in adjudication proceedings between employer and main contractor, the adjudicator finds that the main contractor's work was defective and that work was carried out by a subcontractor, such an award would bind the sub-contractor. If in adjudication proceedings between the employer and the main contractor, the adjudicator finds that the engineer's design is unsafe, the engineer will be bound by such decision as against the employer as if it had been made in adjudication proceedings to which he had been party. This provision may not always be workable, for example, if no reasoned award is given it may not be possible to ascertain what the adjudicator has found or apportion liability as between parties. Further, such a provision may be held to be a restriction on the disputes that may be referred to adjudication in contravention of s 108(1). This is because the sub-contractor in one case and the engineer in the other are denied the right to refer to adjudication a dispute about whether the works were defective in one case or the design unsafe in the other. On the other hand such provision may be held to do no more than define the substantive obligations of the parties over which they are free to adjudicate.

---

53   It may only be extended after referral of the dispute. See s 108(2).
54   By analogy with arbitration. See *The Eastern Saga* [1984] 3 All ER 835.
55   If a power of attorney can be effective to enable time to be extended in advance of referral in order to facilitate multi-party adjudication, it can also be effective for no purpose other than to delay the adjudication proceedings. It is unlikely to be a device viewed with favour by the courts.

---

# 6

# The Scheme For
# Construction Contracts

## 6.1　Introduction

### 6.1.1　The Scheme

By s 114(1) of the Act, the Minister is under obligation by regulations to make the Scheme for Construction Contracts providing for matters referred to in the preceding sections of Pt II of the Act (including s 108). The Minister means, for England and Wales, the Secretary of State and for Scotland, the Lord Advocate.[1] There is one Scheme for England and Wales and another for Scotland although the provision made in the two Schemes is similar save where differences are necessitated by differences between the law or procedure of Scotland and that of England and Wales. Regulations pursuant to s 114(1) were laid in draft before Parliament on 18 December 1997 and re-laid on 12 January 1998 and were debated in the House of Commons on 17 February 1998 and in the House of Lords on 27 February 1998. The commencement date was 6 March 1998 and the Act and the Scheme[2] came into force on 1 May 1998.

The body of SI No 649 of 1998 provides that the Order contained therein may be cited as 'The Scheme for Construction Contracts (England and Wales) Regulations 1998'[3] (hereafter the 'Regulations') and the provisions in the Schedule to the Regulations shall be the Scheme for Construction Contracts (hereafter the Scheme) for the purposes of s 114 of the Act.[4] The Regulations came into force on 1 May 1998.[5] The Regulations contain a Schedule which is divided into two parts— Pt 1 containing the Scheme in so far as it relates to adjudication and Pt II containing the Scheme in so far as it relates to other matters under the Act.[6] Where a construction contract does not comply with the requirements of s 108(1)–(4) of the Act, the adjudication provisions in Pt 1 of the Schedule to the Regulations will apply by way of implied terms of the contract concerned.[7]

### 6.1.2　Implied terms

If a construction contract fails to make any provision at all for adjudication, the Scheme applies by way of implied terms as the sole right of adjudication under the contract. If a contract makes provision for adjudication, which provision fails to comply with the requirements of s 108(1)–(4), the Scheme equally applies by way of implied terms of the contract. However, there is nothing in the Act to suggest that in this case the express contractual adjudication terms do not also apply.[8] In these circumstances, the implied terms of the Scheme lie alongside express adjudication terms which may be different in material respects. By ordinary contractual analysis it is not permissible to imply terms inconsistent with express terms. However, the Act requires the Scheme to apply by way of implied terms, without addressing the effect this may have on existing express terms, with the potential consequence that there may be inconsistent express and implied terms.[9]

### 6.1.3  Interrelationship between contractual and Scheme adjudication

On one view it is a failure in drafting the Act that s 114(4) does not expressly provide that in the event of the applicability of the Scheme, any non compliant contractual adjudication regime ceases to have effect and the sole applicable adjudication procedure is under the Scheme. On another, it is not intrinsically inconsistent with the ideology of the Act if a party with a dispute in any particular case has a choice of which adjudication procedure to adopt, namely, the express contractual adjudication procedure or the Scheme. It is not the purpose of the Act to impose the statutory regime upon the parties—it is there for them if they wish. They may follow whatever regime suits them and be bound by the outcome of that regime.

However, whilst the parties are free to agree otherwise, in circumstances where the Scheme (and presumably also the contractual adjudication procedure) is intended to be a coherent whole, there is no justification for the Scheme adjudicator looking beyond the provisions of the Scheme to the detail of the express contractual adjudication procedure. If this is correct, the Scheme provides a self-contained adjudication regime not to be supplemented by individual adjudication provisions from the contract.

### 6.1.4  Relationship between adjudicator and the parties

The provisions of the Scheme take effect as implied terms of the contract between the parties to the dispute. They do not, necessarily, operate in the contract, if any, between the parties and the adjudicator. It is therefore the case that the parties and the adjudicator should expressly agree between them such matters as remuneration and immunity from suit, and any other matter which either the adjudicator or the parties regard as a matter of importance in their relationship.[10] In the absence of any such agreement, the adjudicator, if he wishes to take advantage of any terms appearing in the construction contract (including those incorporated by way of implied terms by the Scheme) will often be able to argue that his contract with the parties, by implication, was to act as adjudicator in accordance with the contract and on its terms.

### 6.1.5  Scotland

It is not the purpose of this book to consider any aspect of Scottish law or distinguish it from the law of England and Wales. The Scheme and the Exculsion Order applicable in Scotland (s 34 of the Scheme for Construction Contracts (Scotland) Regulations 1998 (SI No 687) and s 33 of the Construction Contracts Exclusion Order 1998 (SI No 686)) are in very similar terms to those applicable in England and Wales and deliberately so. The differences, where significant in effect, are justified either by differences between the two legal systems or by different results from the Scottish consultation process. It is not intended to analyse the law of Scotland in order to set the Scottish Scheme into context. Scottish readers will take the reasoning and analysis in this book and apply it as demanded by their law.

---

1   Section 114(3).
2   SI No 649 of 1998.
3   Regulations, s 1(1).
4   Regulations, s 4.
5   Regulations, s 1, which provides that the regulations shall come into force at the end of the period of eight weeks beginning with the day on which it is made (the commencement date). The commencement date was 6 March 1998 (see the Commencement Order SI No 650 of 1998) and therefore the Scheme came into force on 1 May 1998
6   See s 3 of the Regulations.
7   Section 114(4) of the Act.
8   Whilst it probably follows that any contractual adjudication provision which purports to oust or diminish the effect of the statutory right to adjudication will be of no effect, it does not follow that a non-compliant adjudication procedure does so. It would be a difficult if not impossible contractual analysis that it is an implied term of the contract that in the event that the Scheme applies the express contractual adjudication provisions do not. However, there is no reason why such result should not be expressly provided for by contract.
9   If the analysis below is correct that there may in these circumstances be two separate adjudication procedures for a party to choose from, differences between the two procedures may be just that, namely, differences and not inconsistencies.
10  See, for example, imunity from suit and remuneration.

---

## 6.2   The nature of delegated legislation

### 6.2.1   Challenging delegated legislation

The Regulations are delegated legislation. Delegated legislation is inferior to primary legislation in the form of Acts of Parliament. If validly made, delegated legislation has the full force and effect of an Act of Parliament such that if it requires something to be done, the consequences of failure to do it are as if an Act of Parliament had required that thing to be done. A major difference between delegated legislation and an Act of Parliament is that delegated legislation may be challenged before the courts. Constitutionally, Acts of Parliament cannot be challenged.

There are a number of bases upon which delegated legislation may be challenged. Some are formal, such as that the delegated legislation concerned was not passed in the manner required by its enabling statute. Others are substantive, for example, that the delegated legislation is *ultra vires* the enabling legislation. When interpreting delegated legislation, the overriding principle is that the delegated legislation should be construed, if possible, in the light of the enabling Act of Parliament, such that it is not inconsistent with its substantive provisions and is in conformity with its enabling power.

### 6.2.2   Interpreting the Scheme

A court, faced with two rival interpretations of a piece of delegated legislation, can be expected to favour the one most likely to be justified as *intra vires* the enabling Act. If it is not possible to construe it in this manner and the inevitable conclusion is that it is inconsistent with the enabling Act or goes beyond the power conferred upon the delegated legislation maker, it will, to this extent, be void. So, in one Australian case[11] an Act of Parliament conferred power to make regulations relating to the manner of carrying out construction works such as to make them safe. The regulations in fact passed imposed an absolute obligation to make construction works safe and it was held that the terms of this delegated legislation went beyond the powers conferred by the enabling statute and the delegated legislation was void.

The rationale of the Scheme is to provide, for those construction contracts which do not do so for themselves, a workable procedure in compliance with s 108 of the Act for the adjudication of disputes arising under construction contracts. It is necessarily the case that the Scheme is significantly more detailed than the Act and makes provision which, whilst not inconsistent with the Act, is not required by it. This will not render the Scheme *ultra vires*. It must be noted, however, that the power granted to the Minister pursuant to s 114(1) of the Act is limited to making a scheme containing provision about 'the matters referred to in the preceding provisions' of Pt II of the Act. If and to the extent that the Scheme goes beyond this scope, it is void.

### 6.2.3   Partial invalidity

If the Scheme is *ultra vires* the Act in any respect, it will not necessarily render the whole Scheme void such that the Act as a whole is unworkable. Partial invalidity of delegated legislation has been recognised[12] and it is probably not even necessary to be able to effect a textual deletion of offending material (the blue pencil test) for the severance of *ultra vires* text from that which is *intra vires*. The courts have no power to substitute for what has been struck out of delegated legislation as *ultra vires* some other provision which the delegated legislation maker could have but did not provide.

It is unlikely that a court will view favourably any suggestion that the Scheme is *ultra vires* the Act.[13] However, if this conclusion is inevitable, the courts will not shy away from it. It is only upon close consideration of the Scheme interpreted in the light of the Act that any possible grounds of *ultra vires* may be substantiated.[14] It follows that it is the Scheme which must be interpreted in the light of the Act and not the other way round. Therefore, it is not permissible to look to the terms of the Scheme to aid construction of or resolve ambiguities in the Act.

### 6.2.4   Power to amend the Scheme

The provisions of the Scheme constitute a fully workable adjudication procedure. However, the content of the provisions may in some cases be undesirable for any particular contract. This is unsurprising. The Scheme was intended to be a last resort, necessary if the mandatory provisions of the Act were to have any teeth, but applicable only where the parties had failed to make their own adjudication provision compliant with s 108. The Scheme must necessarily cover a very broad range of circumstances and the consequences of this may be that it is not entirely appropriate for any. This is not a criticism of the Scheme so much as a statement of what the Scheme was intended to and must necessarily achieve.

There is no reason why, in any particular case, the parties should not agree specific amendments to the Scheme, which amendments may be agreed after the dispute has arisen or in the construction contract. If amendments to the Scheme are included in the construction contract, the Scheme will be incorporated by reference into the contract and it, as amended, will apply as an express contractual adjudication procedure (and not as implied terms pursuant to s 114(4) of the Act). The amendments agreed should not derogate from the statutory minimum requirements made by s 108 of the Act. If they do, the proper analysis of the contract may be that the contractual adjudication scheme is not compliant with s 108 of the Act and the Scheme in its entirety, and unamended, applies (by reason of s 114(4) of the Act).

---

11  *Utah Construction and Engineering Pty Ltd v Pataky* (NSW) [1966] AC 629.
12  See, for example, *Daymond v Plymouth City Council* [1976] AC 609. See also cases cited in Sir William Wade and Christopher Forsyth, *Administrative Law*, 7th edn (1994), pp 885ff.
13  There is an argument that a provision of the Scheme which might otherwise be *ultra vires* the Act is not so by reason of s 114(4) of the Act which provides that the Scheme is to take effect as implied terms of the contract. There can be no question that implied terms are *ultra vires*. However, this argument overlooks the fundamental objection that it is only by reason of incorporation into the Scheme of such a term that it becomes an implied term of the contract and its very inclusion into the Scheme, as opposed to the effect of its inclusion, is what is challenged.
14  No attempt is made in this book to examine the provisions of the Scheme in detail for the purposes of assessing whether they are *ultra vires* the Act.

---

## 6.3  Consequences of non-compliance with the scheme

Section 114(4) of the Act states that the Scheme takes effect as implied terms of the contract. This is probably sufficient to oust any suggestion that the Scheme creates statutory duties—the obligation to comply with the Scheme remains a contractual one. As such, the consequences of breach are to be analysed as the consequences of breach of any other contractual provision. Damages for breach might, in appropriate circumstances,[15] flow from the failure of one party to comply with a mandatory provision of the Scheme. A more practical sanction will be that the party in default may find adverse inferences drawn against him in consequence of his default and/or the adjudicator may proceed to an award without his co-operation.

Many of the issues referred to in this chapter have been dealt with substantively in previous chapters or the following chapter and are covered briefly here solely to explain how the Scheme addresses them. Reference to other parts of this work is recommended.

---

15  The circumstances will be rare.

## 6.4 Commencing adjudication

### 6.4.1 Notice of adjudication

The Scheme provides that any party to a construction contract ('the referring party') may give written notice ('the notice of adjudication') of his intention to refer any dispute arising under the contract to adjudication (para 1(1)). The Scheme, but not the Act, requires the notice to be in writing. The notice of adjudication must be given to every other party to the contract (para 1(2)). This is not a requirement of the Act which, whilst not express on this point, would seem to require only that notice of adjudication be given to the other party to the dispute.

The notice of adjudication is to set out briefly the nature and a brief description of the dispute and the parties involved (para 1(3)(a)). It must also set out details of where and when the dispute arose (para 1(3)(b)) together with the nature of the redress which is sought (para 1(3)(c)) and the names and addresses of the parties to the contract, including, where appropriate, the addresses which the parties have specified for the giving of notices (para 1(3)(d)). Section 108 of the Act makes no such express provision as is contained within paragraph 1(3) of the Scheme for the detail of the notice of adjudication. However, it would be wise and good practice for parties to contractual adjudication schemes to follow the lead set by the Scheme in this regard.

### 6.4.2 Appointment of adjudicator

The Scheme imposes responsibility for the appointment of the adjudicator upon the referring party. Following the giving of a notice of adjudication and subject to any agreement between the parties to the dispute as to who shall act as adjudicator, the referring party is to obtain the appointment of an adjudicator by steps taken in the following order (para 2):
(a) the person, if any, specified in the contract;
(b) if no such person exists, or if that person is unable or unwilling to act, the nominating body (if any) specified in the contract should be asked to select an adjudicator;
(c) an adjudicator nominating body should be asked to select an adjudicator.

An adjudicator-nominating body is a body (not being a natural person and not being a party to the dispute) which holds itself out publicly as a body which will select an adjudicator when requested to do so by a referring party (para 2(3)). There is no pre-defined list of the authorities capable of nominating adjudicators pursuant to the Scheme. In practice, it is likely to be the professional bodies of the professional disciplines involved in the construction industry, together with the dispute resolution bodies who fulfil this role.[16]

Any person requested to act as adjudicator must indicate whether or not he is willing to act within two days of receiving the request (para 2(2)). Any nominating body or adjudicator nominating body requested to select an adjudicator must communicate its selection to the referring party within five days of receiving the request (para 5(1)). Since any such person or body will not be party to the contract of which the Scheme forms implied terms, this provision can hardly be binding upon such person or body.[17] However, it is likely that most such people and bodies will, in a desire to act professionally, comply with this requirement whenever possible. Notwithstanding, there is a simple expedient to avoid inconvenience from unnecessary delay caused by the tardy reply of persons or bodies asked to act as or select adjudicators—appoint someone else in accordance with para 5(2) or 6(1).

The request for the appointment of an adjudicator is to be accompanied by a copy of the notice of adjudication (para 3).

### 6.4.3   Referral of dispute

The dispute is to be referred to the adjudicator in writing (the 'referral notice') within seven days of the notice of adjudication (para 7(1)). This will not always be possible, for example, where it has taken longer than seven days for the appointment of an adjudicator.

The referral notice shall be accompanied by copies of or relevant extracts from the construction contract and such other documents as the referring party intends to rely on (para 7(2)). 'Documents' in this paragraph are not limited to contemporary documents such as correspondence, site meeting minutes, dayworks sheets etc but include documents specifically prepared for the adjudication such as statements of witnesses and experts reports. In practical terms there is little sanction if the referring party submits additional documents at a later stage and in many cases this will be necessary to deal with points specifically raised by the other party to the dispute. Hardship to the defending party may be avoided by the adjudicator exercising his powers pursuant to para 15.[18] Paragraph 7(2) ensures that valuable time from a very short timetable will not be wasted while the referring party prepares the basic documents which he could have and should have prepared before he commenced the adjudication. At the same time as the documents are sent to the adjudicator, they must be sent to every other party to the dispute (para 7(3)).

---

16   RICS, RIBA etc as well as bodies such as the Official Referees Solicitor's Association, the Chartered Institute of Arbitrators and the Academy of Construction Adjudicators.

17   Unless, contrary to the view expressed above, the Scheme constitutes a statutory and not just a contractual duty.

18   See para **6.8.11**.

---

## 6.5   The adjudicator

### 6.5.1   Natural person

Any person requested or selected to act as adjudicator shall be a natural person acting in his personal capacity and shall not be an employee of any of the parties to the dispute (para 4). What constitutes acting in a personal capacity has not been made clear in the Scheme, although earlier drafts of the Scheme prohibited adjudicators from acting as employee, representative or partner of any partnership, firm, company or other body corporate.

The requirement that the adjudicator be a natural person and that he act in a personal capacity might prevent many individuals with valuable experience from acting. Many experienced individuals will be employees of firms, companies or partnerships. Individuals acting in their personal capacity will not be entitled to call upon the professional indemnity insurance maintained by their employer in the event that it is needed. Furthermore, if an employee is released by his firm to spend time on an adjudication, the question of that employee's liability to account to the firm for fees received arises. If the employee is under an obligation to account to the firm for fees received, it may be that the correct analysis of the arrangement is that he is not in fact acting in his personal capacity at all but as representative or employee of his firm. The circumstances in which a firm would be willing to release a valued employee to adjudicate upon a dispute without remuneration will be rare.

To disallow a firm from acting as adjudicator may remove the benefit potentially available from multi disciplinary adjudicators.

### 6.5.2   Interest

Any person requested or selected to act as adjudicator shall declare any interest, financial or otherwise, in any matter relating to the dispute (para 4). This provision is intended to make the adjudicator's interest in the adjudication transparent but does not prohibit him from acting. He remains entitled to act but must act impartially and is at all times subject to removal by agreement of the parties (para 11). For reasons given elsewhere in this book, the nature of an adjudicator's interest may render his award more open to challenge on the grounds that he may not have acted impartially. However, merely because the proposed adjudicator declares an interest pursuant to para 4 does not mean that any party to the dispute has any entitlement to have him removed or otherwise challenge the validity of his appointment. No objection to the appointment of an adjudicator by any party shall invalidate the adjudicator's appointment or any award he may make (para 10).

## 6.6   Resignation and removal of adjudicator

### 6.6.1   Resignation

An adjudicator may resign at any time on giving notice in writing to the parties to the dispute (para 9(1)). His entitlement to fees in this case will depend upon the terms of the contract, if any, entered into with the parties. The Scheme makes express provision for payment of the adjudicator's fees upon resignation in only two circumstances:[19]

(a) if the adjudicator resigns because a dispute varies significantly from the dispute referred to him in the referral notice and for that reason he is not competent to decide it;

(b) if the adjudicator resigns because the dispute is the same or substantially the same as one which has previously been referred to adjudication and a decision has been taken in that adjudication.

In either case, the adjudicator is entitled to be paid such reasonable amount as he may determine by way of fees and expenses reasonably incurred by him (para 9(4)). This provision is probably not sufficiently wide to entitle the adjudicator to cancellation fees and if he wishes to ensure that the time he has written out of his diary for the adjudication should not be completely without remuneration, he should make express provision for cancellation fees in his agreement with the parties. The adjudicator is entitled to make an apportionment of how his fees are to be paid, for example, he may order the claimant to pay all the fees where the claimant has misrepresented the nature of the dispute. Notwithstanding such apportionment, the parties remain jointly and severally liable therefor (para 9(4)).

As regards (a), if a dispute differs from that referred to the adjudicator, he has no jurisdiction to decide it in the absence of agreement between the parties.[20] Furthermore, it will be rare that an adjudicator will be incompetent to decide the dispute. Lawyer arbitrators have often to decide disputes concerning the technicalities of engineering, architecture or quantity surveying. Unless these arbitrators are to be said to be incompetent, there is no reason why adjudicators should not demonstrate the same level of competence and flexibility.

As regards (b), if the dispute is the same or substantially the same as one which has previously been referred to adjudication and a decision has been taken in that adjudication, the adjudicator must resign (para 9(2)). In this case, a decision which binds the parties has already been taken and the adjudicator should not assist the parties, or one of them, in attempting to breach the obligation to be bound by the first adjudicator's decision.

Where the adjudicator resigns for any reason other than in the circumstances of (b) above, the referring party may serve a fresh notice and commence a fresh adjudication in accordance with paras 2–7 (para 9(3)(a)). If requested by the new adjudicator and in so far as reasonably practicable, the parties shall supply the new adjudicator with copies of all documents that were made available to the previous adjudicator (para 9(3)(b)).

## 6.6.2   Removal

The parties to the dispute may at any time revoke the adjudicator's appointment by agreement (para 11(1)). There is no requirement for notice in writing. In this event the parties are liable for the adjudicator's reasonable fees, as determined by him, and his actual expenses. The parties are liable to pay those fees and expenses in such proportions as directed by the adjudicator (para 11(1)) but they remain jointly and severally liable for any fees outstanding (para 11(1)).

It is strange that where the adjudicator's appointment may be revoked only by agreement between the parties, that agreement should not also be the primary determinant for liability to pay the adjudicator's fees and expenses. However, the proper analysis of this provision of the Scheme should be that the joint and several liability is liability of the parties as between them and the adjudicator (assuming no contractual provision to the contrary between the parties and the adjudicator) but as between themselves, the parties may make such arrangement for the payment of the adjudicator's fees as they see fit.

Where revocation of the appointment of the adjudicator is due to the default or misconduct of the adjudicator, the parties shall not be liable to pay the adjudicator's fees and expenses (para 11(2)). The Scheme provides no guidance as to what amounts to default or misconduct. In the context of adjudication pursuant to the Act it is likely that save in exceptional cases, a failure by the adjudicator to comply with the stringent timetable for the delivery of his award will amount to default, if not misconduct. Acting in good faith beyond his jurisdiction may or may not amount to default or misconduct and the issue may be determined in any particular case as a question of fact and degree.

It is a dangerous analogy to look at the authorities concerning an arbitrator's misconduct, as so much of the material arises against the background of arbitrators exercising judicial functions whilst acting in an adversarial role. The adjudicator will, of course, often be exercising inquisitorial functions, whether or not he is acting judicially.

---

19  See para 8(4) for fees of the adjudicator after consolidation of disputes.
20  See para 4.2.13.

---

## 6.7  Duties of the adjudicator

### 6.7.1  Impartiality

The adjudicator must act impartially in carrying out his duties (para 12(a)). The duty to act impartially reflects the duty set out in s 108(2)(*e*) of the Act and there is in the Scheme, as in the Act, no guidance as to what is required in the performance of this duty. However, the duty to act impartially is fleshed out by para 17, which provides that the adjudicator must consider any relevant information submitted to him by any of the parties to the dispute and must make available to them any information to be taken into account in reaching his decision.

Paragraph 17 prevents the adjudicator from ignoring information submitted by a party and requires him to allow the parties access to information submitted either by one of them or obtained by him in the course of his exercising inquisitorial powers. It is only if the information is to be taken into account in reaching the decision that the adjudicator must make it available to the parties. This probably does not mean that he must make it available only if it is positively accepted. Even if information is rejected or regarded as insufficiently proved, it is likely that the adjudicator must equally make it available to the parties, as the rationale of this provision is to allow the parties the opportunity to comment upon such information, and their comment may affect the adjudicator's decision as to whether to accept or reject it or as to whether it is sufficiently proved.

### 6.7.2  Application of law

The adjudicator must reach his decision in accordance with any relevant terms of the contract and in accordance with the applicable law in relation to the contract (para 12(a)). He must not act as *aimable compositeur* nor rewrite the contract between the parties. He must not decide the dispute on the basis of his idea of what would be a commercially reasonable solution pending final resolution of the dispute in court or arbitration, nor must he constitute himself or anybody else trustee stakeholder or make interlocutory orders for the interim preservation of property etc. He must decide the dispute in accordance with the parties' legal rights and obligations.

### 6.7.3 Avoiding unnecessary expense

The adjudicator must avoid incurring unnecessary expense (para 12(b)). This provision is a worthy statement of intent. However, it carries the risk that a party who disagrees with the way the adjudicator has conducted the adjudication may claim that the adjudicator has failed to avoid unnecessary expense, which failure constitutes default, misconduct or breach of contract, entitling him to renege from liability to pay the adjudicator's fees.

## 6.8 Powers of the adjudicator

### 6.8.1 Taking the initiative

The adjudicator may take the initiative in ascertaining the fact and law necessary for determining the dispute (para 13). He is thus empowered to take an inquisitorial approach to his task and need not confine himself to adversarial procedures adopted in court or arbitration.[21]

### 6.8.2 Procedure

The adjudicator is to decide the procedure to be followed in the adjudication (para 13). In circumstances where the obligation to adjudicate is, as between the parties, a contractual one and the relationship between the parties and the adjudicator is contractual, there appears to be no reason why the parties should not, in spite of para 13, agree procedure for themselves—which agreement should override any determination of the adjudicator. He has specific powers to determine procedure as set out in paras 13(a)–(h) of the Scheme but these provisions should not be regarded as exhaustive.

### 6.8.3 Documents

The adjudicator may request any party to the contract to supply him with such documents as he may reasonably require, including written statements from any party to the contract supporting or supplementing the referral notice and any other documents accompanying the referral notice (para 13(a)). The adjudicator can request the parties to supply him with existing documents so that this power is analogous to a court's power to order the disclosure of documents. He may also direct the parties to prepare a document such as a statement of his case, statement of evidence etc.

### 6.8.4 Language

The adjudicator may decide the language or languages to be used in the adjudication and whether a document should be translated and if so by whom (para 13(b)). Power to order translations may be a useful tool, if one that is used rarely.

### 6.8.5   Questioning

The adjudicator may meet and question any of the parties to the contract and their representatives (para 13(c)). This paragraph does not specify whether the questioning of the parties or their representatives must take place in the presence of the other parties to the adjudication. It is suggested that this is not a requirement which could easily have been but was not, made express.[22] The terms of para 17 of the Scheme make it clear that the adjudicator should not take into account information which has not been made available to the other parties to the dispute. This will include information obtained during the meeting and questioning referred to in para 13(c). There is, in these circumstances, no need to restrict the adjudicator to meetings and questioning in the presence of all the parties and to do so could undermine the general power of the adjudicator to take the initiative in ascertaining the facts and the law.

This paragraph cannot confer power upon the adjudicator to question the parties legal representatives without consent. Any such power would be fundamentally objectionable as contrary to legal professional privilege, honoured in every other tribunal in the country.

The power to question technical representatives without consent of the parties will often also be objectionable. The adjudicator, however, has no compulsive powers and if a representative chooses not to be questioned, there is nothing the adjudicator can do. He should be very slow indeed to draw adverse inferences against a party whose representative will not be questioned unless that party himself has control over the representative, for example, if he is an employee

### 6.8.6   Site visits, tests and experiments

Subject to obtaining any necessary consent from third parties, the adjudicator may make such site visits and inspections as he considers appropriate, whether accompanied by the parties or not (para 13(d)), and he may carry out any tests and experiments (para 13(e)). It is obvious that if property, whether it be the site of the works or not, is in the possession or ownership of a third party, the adjudicator requires the consent of that third party before entering upon or dealing with that property. If he fails to obtain such consent, he may be liable for trespass or some other tort, but he has, as between the parties to the adjudication, the right to make such visits, inspections, tests and experiments.[23]

### 6.8.7   Submissions

The adjudicator may obtain and consider such representations and submissions as he requires (para 13(f)). Although the Scheme does not specifically require the adjudicator to allow each party to reply to the representations and submissions made by the other, it is suggested that it is implicit in his overriding duty to act impartially that he should do so. Whether the representations and submissions of the parties are to be oral or in writing is within the proper domain of the adjudicator to decide. Subject to paragraph 17 and the adjudicator's duty of impartiality, there is no requirement that the representations be made in the presence of or copied to all parties to the dispute.

### 6.8.8  Experts and advisers

The adjudicator has the authority to appoint experts, assessors or legal advisers without the consent of the parties provided he has notified them of his intention so to do (para 13(f)). However, if the parties agree that he should not appoint such experts, assessors or legal advisers, his authority implied into the contract by the terms of para 13(f) will be withdrawn.

### 6.8.9  Timetable, length of submissions and deadlines

The adjudicator may give directions as to the timetable for the adjudication and deadlines or limits to the length of written documents or oral representations (para 13(g)). So, the adjudicator presiding over an oral hearing can enforce the operation of a 'chess clock' procedure, whereby each side has a finite period of time for the making of submissions. The adjudicator can, in the interests of speed and economy, limit the length of written submissions and impose deadlines upon the parties for the submission of any document or other action to be taken in the adjudication.

### 6.8.10  General powers

Paragraph 13(h) gives the adjudicator extensive powers to give directions relating to the conduct of the adjudication. The adjudicator's power to issue directions relating to the conduct of the adjudication entitles him to decide such matters as: the order of evidence, and submissions; if, where and when any oral hearing will be held; whether written representations are to be supplied in hard copy or on disk etc. He may order the parties to hire a room for the adjudication hearing and arrange for the engagement of transcript writers. This power, contained within para 13(h), makes the adjudicator master of his own procedure.

### 6.8.11  Sanctions for failure to comply

There is a general obligation in para 14 to comply with any request or direction of the adjudicator. If, without showing sufficient cause, a party fails to comply, the adjudicator has the power to continue the adjudication in the absence of that party or in the absence of any document requested (para 15(a)), draw such inferences from failure to comply as may, in the adjudicator's opinion be justified (para 15(b)) or make a decision on the basis of the information before him, attaching such weight as he thinks fit to any evidence submitted to him outside any period he may have requested or directed (para 15(c)). Failure to comply with the adjudicator's directions will not allow one party to thwart the adjudication procedure.

Paragraph 15 confers power on the adjudicator to take the steps identified in subparas (a)–(c) only if a party has failed to comply with an order 'without showing sufficient cause.' There is no guidance in the Scheme as to how the adjudicator is to exercise this power. What amounts to 'sufficient cause' must obviously be decided on a case by case basis and in the light of the circumstances prevailing. On one view, sufficient cause may be shown where a party is unable to comply with an order or direction by reason, for example, of unavailability of staff, inability to contact relevant personnel who may have left the employ of that party or inability to retrieve relevant documents from archive in sufficient time. On this view it will only be inappropriate to apply sanctions for failure to comply with an adjudicator's order where the failure is clearly beyond the control of the defaulting party. In the context of adjudication, these causes of inability to comply with the adjudicator's order are likely to be met with more frequently that in the context of other dispute resolution techniques given the short timetable for the adjudication procedure. However, an adjudicator has no power unilaterally to prolong the process, however reasonable and compelling his desire to do so, in order to enable a party to comply with his directions. In these circumstances he may have no choice but to exercise one or more of the powers set out in para 15 (a)–(c).

In fact, it may be that it matters little how 'sufficient cause' is interpreted in para 15, as the adjudicator's powers are permissive only and not mandatory and the adjudicator probably has equivalent powers by reason of his status as such even without para 15 of the Scheme.

---

21  See para 4.4.
22  Contrast, however, the wording of para 13(d) which makes it clear that the adjudicator may make site visits and inspections whether or not in the presence of the parties.
23  The words 'subject to' in paras 13(d) and (e) suggest that any necessary third party consent is a condition precedent to the adjudicator's entitlement as against the parties to make the site visits, inspections, tests and experiments referred to. However, while the adjudicator may have a third party to answer to if he makes such visits, inspections, tests and experiments without consent, it should have no bearing on the effectiveness of the adjudicator's award as between the parties.

---

## 6.9   The adjudicator's decision

### 6.9.1   Time for delivery of decision

The adjudicator must reach his decision not later than 28 days after the referral notice, 42 days after the referral notice if the referring party consents, or such time exceeding 28 days after the referral notice as the parties to the dispute may, after giving the referral notice, agree (para 19(1)).

Where the adjudicator fails for any reason to reach his decision in accordance with para 19(1), the parties may commence adjudication afresh and shall seek the appointment of a different adjudicator (para 19(2)(a)) and, if requested by the new adjudicator and in so far as reasonably practicable, they must supply him with copies of all documents which they made available to the previous adjudicator (para 19(2)(b)).

It will often be misconduct or default if the adjudicator fails to reach his decision in accordance with the restrictive timetable prescribed by the Scheme. In exceptional cases, such as unexpected illness, failure by the adjudicator to comply with the timetable cannot be said to be misconduct or default but the parties are free to commence adjudication afresh in any event. In this case, whether they do so is a decision which should be taken in the light of a number of prevailing considerations, such as the likely continued delay in obtaining a decision from the first adjudicator, the parties' continued liability for his fees and commercial considerations, such as whether the result of the adjudication is likely to be the desired one.

The adjudicator must, as soon as he has reached his decision, deliver a copy of that decision to each of the parties to the contract (para 19(3)). The adjudicator is entitled to no contractual lien pursuant to the Scheme.

### 6.9.2   Obligation to make a decision

Paragraph 20 sets out the adjudicator's overriding duty—which is to make a decision on the matters in dispute. The opening words of para 20 are obscure. The adjudicator may 'take into account' any 'other' matters which the parties to the dispute agree should be within the scope of the adjudication or which are matters under the contract which he considers are necessarily connected with the dispute.

If the parties agree that matters other than those referred should be within the scope of the adjudication, they may give the adjudicator jurisdiction to make a decision upon them. However, it is not the case that the adjudicator may decide matters 'necessarily connected with the dispute' if those matters have not been referred to him for decision. It is suggested in this case that he may take them into account, in the sense of allowing them to bear upon his decision, but he should not make a decision in relation to them which purports to be an enforceable adjudicator's decision.

Paragraph 20 lists three powers that the adjudicator may exercise under the general banner of deciding the matters in dispute. They are dealt with in turn below.

### 6.9.3   Power to review certificates

The adjudicator may open up, revise and review any decision taken or any certificate given by any person referred to in the contract unless the contract states that the decision or certificate is final and conclusive (para 20(a)).

So, if a certificate is stated in the contract to be final and conclusive, the adjudicator has no power to revise and review it pursuant to the Scheme. However, if a certificate is stated to be final and conclusive only conditionally,[24] it is not clear in what circumstances the adjudicator has power to revise and review it. A certificate is conclusive conditionally if the contract provides that it is conclusive only in certain circumstances, for example, if not challenged in arbitration within a specified period of time. In this case, there are two alternative constructions of para 20(a) of the Scheme:
(1)   The contract does not state a certificate to be final and conclusive unless it is final and conclusive in all circumstances and for all purposes.

(2)  The contract states a certificate to be final and conclusive once the condition for its conclusiveness has been satisfied.

If (1) is the correct construction, an adjudicator may revise and review a conditionally conclusive certificate notwithstanding that it has become final and conclusive under the contract, and notwithstanding that no arbitrator or court can review it. If (2) is correct, the adjudicator can revise and review such a certificate before it has become conclusive, but not after. It is suggested that (2) is the preferable construction, as it more closely honours the parties' intentions as set out in the contract and is less likely to result in the Scheme being held to be *ultra vires* the Act.

A contract which attempts to oust jurisdiction from an adjudicator but leaves certificates to be opened up, reviewed and revised in arbitration, does not 'state that the ... certificate is final and conclusive' so as to deprive the adjudicator of power pursuant to para 20(a) of the Scheme.

Pursuant to s 114(1) of the Act, the Secretary of State's power is one to make a Scheme containing provision about the matters referred to in the preceding provisions of Pt II of the Act. These matters include adjudicating upon a dispute arising under a construction contract. Reviewing and revising certificates under construction contracts may not be a simple matter of deciding a dispute. In some cases, where a court has power to review and revise a decision or certificate and determine a dispute in relation to it, the adjudicator should have power to do likewise. However, in those circumstances in which a court would have no such jurisdiction,[25] it is difficult to see how an adjudicator can be clothed with such authority under the banner of deciding a dispute.[26]

### 6.9.4  Payment

The adjudicator may decide that any of the parties to the dispute is liable to make a payment under the contract, whether in sterling or some other currency and, subject to s 111(4) of the Act, when that payment is due and the final date for payment (para 20(b)).

Adjudications seeking the payment of money are likely to be the most common type pursued under the Act and para 20(b) gives the adjudicator express authority to decide that one party is liable to pay the disputed sum. The authority conferred by para 20(b) is only to make decisions about monies due 'under the contract' and may not, therefore, be sufficient to confer power to award damages for breach of contract. However, the opening words of para 20 are general in nature and the particular powers conferred by subparas (a)–(c) are not exhaustive of the adjudicator's powers. He may, therefore, pursuant to his general power, award damages for breach.

Paragraph 20(b) entitles the adjudicator to decide when the payment found to be due is in fact due and the final date for payment. It is beyond the scope of this book to discuss the intricacies and problems arising from the concepts of when a payment is 'due' and the 'final date for payment' as these terms are used in the Act.[27] However, if a payment is not already due when an adjudication is commenced, that payment ought not to have been claimed in the adjudication at all and the final date for payment is one which ought to have been, and may very well have been, expressly catered for in the contract. The adjudicator cannot rewrite the contract in this regard. What is probably meant by para 20(b) is that the adjudicator may adjudicate upon rival contentions as to whether a payment is due and when—pursuant to the contract, the Act and the general law—the final date for payment falls. The adjudicator must of necessity state a period within which the amount awarded by him must be paid.

### 6.9.5   Interest

The adjudicator may decide the circumstances in which and the rates at which and the periods for which simple or compound rates of interest shall be paid, having regard to any term of the contract relating to the payment of interest (para 20(c)). If the contract makes specific provision for the payment of interest the adjudicator should honour the parties' contractual rights and obligations.

In circumstances where the contract is silent on the question of interest, it is not clear whether para 20(c) purports to give and is successful in giving the adjudicator power to award interest, simple, compound or at all. It is suggested that he has such power. On one view, it makes little sense to require the adjudicator to have regard to an express term of the contract that no interest is payable but to allow him to disregard the fact that the parties have made no provision for interest and therefore, following the general law, no interest is payable. However, if para 20(c) means no more than that the adjudicator must honour any contractual provision the parties have or have not made for interest, this paragraph is entirely redundant as the obligation to apply the terms of the contract has been specifically provided for in para 13.

### 6.9.6   Time for compliance

The adjudicator may fix in his award time for compliance with any order he may make. In the absence of any directions as to the time for performance, the parties are required to comply with his award immediately on delivery of his decision 'in accordance with this paragraph' (para 21). It is not immediately clear what 'in accordance with this paragraph' means. As para 21 makes no requirements as to the time of delivery of the award or the form or content of the award when delivered, it is tempting to conclude that the words 'in accordance with this paragraph' are mere verbiage.

The adjudicator's power to fix a time for performance of the award should be exercised in the light of s 111(4) of the Act, which requires that in certain circumstances a decision of the adjudicator be construed to mean that payment is to be made within seven days. These circumstances are where an effective notice of intention to withhold payment (notice of set off) has been served but the adjudicator has found that the monies withheld should be paid. There is little point in the adjudicator fixing a time for payment in these circumstances other than in accordance with s 111(4).

### 6.9.7   Reasons

If requested by one of the parties to the dispute, the adjudicator shall provide reasons for his decision (para 22). There is no time limit stated within which the

request for reasons must be made and there is therefore no reason to suggest that
the request may not be made at any time whether before or after the decision is
given. The benefits and disadvantages of reasons are discussed elsewhere in this
book.[28]

---

24  For example JCT 80 clause 30.9 and *Crown Estate Commissioners v John Mowlem & Company Ltd*
   (1994) 70 BLR 1.
25  Such cases may still exist notwithstanding the decision in *Beaufort Developments (NI) Ltd v Gil
   bert-Ash Ltd and Others* (House of Lords, 20 May 1998).
26  The risk of *ultra vires* has been significantly reduced by the decision in *Beaufort Developments (NI
   Ltd v Gilbert-Ash Ltd and Others* (House of Lords, 20 May 1998).
27  See s 110 of the Act.
28  See para **5.5.2**.

---

## 6.10   Effects of decision

### 6.10.1   Temporary binding effect

Paragraph 23(2) provides that the decision of the adjudicator is binding upon the
parties and they shall comply with it until the dispute is finally determined by
legal proceedings, by arbitration (if the contract provides for arbitration, or if the
parties agree to arbitration) or by agreement between the parties. This provision
is made in compliance with and to reflect the requirements of s 108(3) of the Act

### 6.10.2   Peremptory orders of the adjudicator

In his decision, the adjudicator may, if he thinks fit, order any of the parties to
comply peremptorily with his decision or any part of it (para 23(1)). What 'per
emptorily' means for the purposes of this paragraph has not been defined and i
not clear. A peremptory court order is one that carries sanctions for failure to
comply. The adjudicator cannot apply sanctions for failure to comply with hi
award as not only is he, after his award, *functus officio*, but he has no compulsive
powers for enforcing compliance.

However, it probably does not matter what 'peremptorily' means for the pur
poses of para 23(1). Whatever it means, and so long as it is clear that a peremp
tory order has been made, the provisions of s 42 of the Arbitration Act 1996 will
become operative (para 24). An adjudicator wishing to ensure that the partie
have the benefits provided by para 24, namely, the applicability of s 42 of the
Arbitration Act 1996, should make clear that his decision, or part of it, is a per
emptory one pursuant to para 23(2) and that it is intended that on failure to com
ply, the courts should have power pursuant to para 24 under s 42 of the Arbitration
Act 1996.

The Scheme does not define what form a peremptory order must take or it
content. A peremptory order should, for the sake of clarity and to avoid misur
derstanding and room for argument, usually state a specific time for compliance
In the absence of a specific time for compliance, it will often be difficult for an

person looking at the order to be confident that it has not been complied with.

### 6.10.3 Court enforcement of peremptory orders

Section 42 of the Arbitration Act 1996 is incorporated into the Scheme by para 24. Paragraph 24(a)–(d) makes such consequential amendment to the provisions of s 42 as is necessary to make it appropriate for use in the context of adjudication rather than arbitration.

Section 42 of the Arbitration Act 1996 gives the court power to make an order requiring a party to comply with a peremptory order of the adjudicator. If the party against whom the order is made continues to be in default of the court order, the court may apply such sanctions as are available for breach of court orders, for example, fine or committal for contempt.

The court's power under s 42 of the Arbitration Act 1996 is intended, in the context of arbitration, to bolster the powers of the arbitration tribunal to enforce interlocutory orders. In the context of adjudication, however, it is clearly intended as an aid to the enforcement of the final award and as such may provide a useful alternative to enforcement by summary proceedings under RSC Ord 14.[29]

However, there is no guidance in the context of arbitration, still less in the context of adjudication, as to the circumstances in which the court should exercise the powers conferred by s 42. It is not the case that the court should exercise its powers merely because an adjudicator's award has been made. A peremptory adjudicator's decision should not be enforced if it was made without jurisdiction, or made after a procedure that was unfair, or even possibly if it was made without taking account of a counterclaim.[30] It is only when authority becomes available upon the proper exercise of the court's powers pursuant to para 24 of the Scheme that the full significance of the paragraph will be known.

No order should be made pursuant to s 42 unless the court is satisfied that there has been a failure to comply with the adjudicator's award within the time prescribed or if no time was prescribed within a reasonable time (s 42(4) of the Arbitration Act 1996). For reasons given previously, it is preferable if the adjudicator states a specific time for compliance with his peremptory award in order to avoid argument as to what constitutes a reasonable time.

The power of the court is exercisable only upon application made either by the adjudicator (upon notice to the parties)[31] or a party to the proceedings with the permission of the adjudicator (upon notice to the other parties).[32] The leave of the court is required for any appeal from a decision of the court under s 42.

### 6.10.4 Objections to paragraph 24

There are at least two objections to the incorporation into the Scheme of s 42 of the Arbitration Act 1996.
(1) If, as would appear to be the case, the purpose of incorporation is to enhance the enforceability of the adjudicator's final award, it is at least arguable that this is not a provision about the matters referred to in the Act such as to be within the power granted to the delegated legislation maker by s 114(1) of the Act.

(2)   It is not clear that it is open to the parties to agree by their contract to confer a power upon a court which power the court does not intrinsically have. Parties to a contract, other than an arbitration agreement, cannot confer jurisdiction upon a court to exercise the powers contained within s 42 of the Arbitration Act 1996. Parties to an arbitration agreement have power to do so only because the Arbitration Act 1996 expressly provides that they have such power. It is not clear that the Scheme is sufficient to confer such power on the parties to adjudications, as the Scheme would appear to have no statutory status but operate only by way of implied terms of the contract.

---

29   Enforcement by summary proceedings under RSC Ord 14 will, in many cases, be fraught with difficulty. See Chapter 7.
30   For example, if the counterclaim was outwith the adjudicator's jurisdiction and the claimant refused to agree to confer such jurisdiction upon the adjudicator.
31   It is not clear why the adjudicator should wish to make such application.
32   Section 42(2)(c) of the Arbitration Act has been deleted by para 24(c) of the Scheme. Thus agreement of the parties that the court should have power under s 42 is not a basis upon which the court derives jurisdiction.

---

## 6.11   The adjudicator's fees

The adjudicator is entitled to determine his own fees and expenses (para 25). His determination must be a reasonable amount by way of fees and expenses reasonably incurred by him (para 25).[33] This provision makes it clear that the adjudicator's fees and expenses must be reasonable, but in circumstances where it is the adjudicator who determines them and there is no procedure under the Scheme for challenging his determination, the safeguard built into the Scheme that the adjudicator may charge only reasonable fees may be more illusory than real. The parties are jointly and severally liable for any sum which remains outstanding following the making of any determination on how the payment shall be apportioned (para 25).

There is no provision for the taxation of the adjudicator's fees and if they are disputed the only procedure for ascertaining whether they are claimed in a correct amount pursuant to para 25 of the Scheme is by claiming/defending the claim in court.

There is no express provision in the Scheme for the adjudicator to exercise a lien on his award pending payment of his fees. On the contrary, there is an express obligation upon the adjudicator pursuant to para 19(3) to deliver a copy of his award to the parties as soon as possible after he has reached his decision. If the adjudicator seeks to exercise a lien, he should ensure that proper provision therefor has been made in the contract between him and the parties.

---

33   In the contract between the adjudicator and the parties the adjudicator can make whatever arrangement he considers appropriate for the payment of his fees and the parties are bound in contract to any agreement they reach with him, regardless of the provisions of para 25 of the Scheme.

## 6.12   Immunity from suit

Paragraph 26 of the Scheme provides immunity from suit to the adjudicator and any employee or agent of the adjudicator in exactly the terms required by s 108(4) of the Act.[34]

## 6.13   Confidentiality

Paragraph 18 of the Scheme imposes an obligation of confidentiality upon the adjudicator and the parties to the dispute not to disclose to any other person any information or documents provided in connection with the adjudication which the supplying party has indicated are to be treated as confidential, except to the extent that it is necessary for the purposes of or, in connection with, the adjudication.

This provision has three important aspects:

(1)   The confidentiality restriction applies only where the party supplying the information or documents has indicated that it is to be treated as confidential. Whilst such indication may be spelt out of surrounding circumstances, it is clearly preferable for parties who wish to maintain confidentiality expressly to require it. The confidentiality restriction does not apply to any information or document in the public domain.

(2)   The restriction does not apply to the extent that disclosure is necessary for the purposes of or in connection with the adjudication. So, for example, if the adjudicator appoints a third party assessor or legal adviser, the restriction does not apply. It will clearly be a question of fact in any particular case whether disclosure is so necessary. It is not clear whether court proceedings, for example, under para 24 of the Scheme or for the enforcement of the award are for the purposes of or in connection with 'the adjudication'. It is suggested that they probably are, but in any event, contractual confidentiality restrictions are of limited effect to evade full disclosure or to defeat a subpoena[35].

(3)   The duty of confidentiality requires only that the parties and the adjudicator shall not disclose to any other person the information or documents referred to. It does not expressly exclude strangers to the dispute from any oral hearings but, as a private procedure, it is within the control of the parties so to do. It would, it is suggested, be a breach of the confidentiality restriction were one party to procure that a stranger attend the hearing without the consent of the other.

---

34  See para **4.5**.
35  See para **5.6**.

---

## 6.14   Representation

Paragraph 16(1) enables any party to the dispute subject to agreement to the contrary and to para 16(2) to be assisted or represented by such advisers or representatives (whether legally qualified or not) as he considers appropriate. There is no professional body with a monopoly upon representation before adjudicators, so a party may be represented by a lawyer, any other professional or any individual, partnership or company as he considers appropriate. Nor is there any limit upon the number of advisers or representatives a party may have.[36] However, para 16(2) provides that where the adjudicator is considering oral evidence or representations, a party to the dispute may not be represented by more than one person, unless the adjudicator gives directions to the contrary.

If para 16(2) is intended to ensure that there is no proliferation of evidence or submissions and that the evidence and submissions are controlled in terms of time, that can be achieved pursuant to para 13(g) and (h) without recourse to the obscure and unnecessarily restrictive terms of para 16(2).

Paragraph 16(2) is obscure because it is not clear precisely what it means. It may mean that the practice of having a leading barrister and a junior at the hearing is not to be permitted without the adjudicator's consent. In the vast majority of adjudications, although not all, this practice would be entirely unnecessary in any event, but as the adjudicator cannot award costs and should have tight control over the procedure, the restriction on representation might achieve little more than amounting to an unwelcome interference with the way a party wishes to conduct its case. Paragraph 16(2) might prevent a party's solicitors instructing a barrister or might restrict the number of technical representatives (experts) a party brings to establish his case.

The adjudicator should give directions under para 16(2) permitting a party to present his case at an oral hearing in any way he considers appropriate, provided that no injustice or inconvenience is thereby caused to the other party. Control of the proceedings may be exercised by means other than by interfering with the party's choice of representation.

## 6.15  Multi-party adjudication

Multi-party adjudication is provided for in para 8 of the scheme. The adjudicator may adjudicate at the same time on more than one dispute arising under the same contract (para 8(1)). The adjudicator may also adjudicate at the same time on related disputes arising under different contracts (para 8(2)). In both cases consent of all the parties to the disputes to be consolidated is required and para 8(2) is applicable whether or not one or more of those parties is a party to those disputes. This wording is obscure but probably means only that for consolidation of disputes pursuant to this paragraph, it is not necessary that any party is a party to all of the disputes to be consolidated. That he is a party to one is sufficient.

In order for the adjudicator to consolidate disputes in this way, it will often be necessary for the parties to the disputes to extend the period within which the adjudicator must reach his decision. This power is conferred by para 8(3) of the Scheme. Consolidation of disputes cannot be achieved unilaterally by one of the parties without consent of the others and it cannot effectively be provided for in advance in the construction contract. This is because there is a statutory maximum period of time for the adjudication procedure to be completed in the absence of agreement to the contrary, and that agreement cannot be contained within the construction contract as it must be reached after the dispute has been referred to adjudication.[37] Agreement after referral will often not be possible as one party may perceive that consolidation is not in his commercial interests.

An adjudicator who is released by reason of the consolidation of disputes before a different adjudicator is entitled to his fees and expenses, determined in accordance with para 25 (para 8(4)).

---

36  There is no provision in the Scheme for the adjudicator to award costs in favour of any party to the dispute. Legal or other professional representatives or advisers are therefore engaged entirely at a party's own expense.
37  See s 108(2)(c) of the Act.

# 7

# Enforcement, Remedies and Challenge

## 7.1 Introduction

### 7.1.1 Contractual right

If the contract is to comply with the requirements of s 108(3) of the Act, it must provide that the decision of the adjudicator is binding until the dispute is finally determined by court proceedings, arbitration or agreement.[1] Such provision imposes upon the parties a contractual obligation to comply with the adjudicator's award.[2] If the Scheme applies it has effect in accordance with s 114(4), as implied contractual obligations. Enforcement of the award will be subject to the same rules and principles as apply to the enforcement of any other contractual right.

### 7.1.2 A form of estoppel

An adjudicator's award cannot give rise to *res judicata*[3] or issue estoppel.[4] However, the contractual provision that the adjudicator's award is binding until overturned means that if an issue is determined by an adjudicator it cannot be reviewed substantively either in proceedings to enforce the award or in further adjudication proceedings. So, a court will not review the substance of the dispute in enforcement proceedings and a defence which fails when raised in adjudication against one claim probably cannot be brought again to defend another. The decision in the first adjudication is binding until the award is overturned and the same facts cannot be adjudicated over again in defence to a series of claims for payment.[5] Equally, a claimant, dissatisfied with the level of the award cannot commence adjudication proceedings afresh in the hope of increasing it. The award can be reviewed substantively in court or arbitration proceedings for the purposes of overturning it.[6]

If the adjudicator makes no decision on a particular issue referred to him by either the claimant or the defendant, the referring party is free to refer it again for decision under another adjudication procedure. If it is not clear whether the adjudicator has made a decision on a particular issue, the practical effect will be that neither party will be able to establish that a decision on it has already been made such as to become binding pursuant to s 108(3). If the adjudicator is under no obligation to supply a reasoned award, it may be impossible to say whether the adjudicator has made a decision upon a particular issue.

---

1   The parties may agree to accept the decision of the adjudicator as finally determining their dispute. Section 108(3).
2   See paras **3.1.4** and **3.1.5**.
3   Available only for court judgments.
4   The adjudication procedure, being of interim effect only, assumes that the issue in dispute may be revisited at a later date. Therefore, issue estoppel is an inappropriate concept in the context of adjudication.
5   This is permitted under Dom/1, cl 24.7.
6   See paras **7.6.1** –**7.6.3**.

---

## 7.2   Enforcement

### 7.2.1   No direct enforcement

An adjudicator's award for the payment of money may not be enforced directly by levying execution upon the unsuccessful party's assets. An adjudicator does not have power to enforce a non-money award with the threat of committal for contempt. A judgment of the court is required if the award is to be enforced.

There is no specific procedure for turning an adjudicator's award into an order of the court for the purposes of enforcement. The procedure set out in s 66 of the Arbitration Act 1996 for direct enforcement of an arbitration award with leave of the court is not available to enforce an adjudicator's award.[7] Nor is there any equivalent, in the context of adjudication, of s 66 of the Arbitration Act 1996.

### 7.2.2   Insolvency procedures

A demand for payment under s 123 or s 268 of the Insolvency Act 1986 may be made in reliance upon an adjudicator's award. This means that the party upon whom the demand is made has 21 days within which to pay the amount demanded. If it is not paid within this time, the claimant may present a petition for the bankruptcy or winding up of the defendant. However, if the claim is contested,[8] the court will not make a bankruptcy or winding up order. If the defendant has no real defence to the claim, the insolvency procedures may be the most effective way to apply pressure for the payment of adjudicators' awards. The insolvency procedures are useful only for the enforcement of liquidated money awards.

### 7.2.3   Full trial on merits

The claimant may commence an action by writ to enforce the adjudicator's award. He may proceed to trial upon the substantive merits of the dispute. If he does so, he will not be relying upon the adjudicator's award already made in his favour, but, if he obtains judgment, he will have a judgment which finally resolves the dispute between the parties. This is unlikely to be an attractive option for a party who is successful in adjudication. It will take many months, if not years, to obtain a judgment from the court after full trial on the substantive merits of the dispute and the adjudicator's award in his favour will have served him nothing.

### 7.2.4 Summary judgment

A party who has been successful in adjudication will usually prefer to commence an action by writ and seek summary judgment. The claim in this case will not be brought on the substantive merits of the dispute but rather on the grounds that the defendant has an obligation pursuant to the contract to comply with the adjudicator's award (*Drake & Skull Engineering Ltd v McLaughlin & Harvey plc* 60 BLR 102 at p 110). The claim is a contractual one like any other. Summary judgment is a procedure designed to enable those plaintiffs with indisputably valid claims to obtain immediate judgment without the need full trial. Summary judgment is appropriate only when the plaintiff's case can be established to be good without investigation of disputed fact.

### 7.2.5 Authorities

There are few authorities dealing with enforcement by summary proceedings or otherwise of an adjudicator's award. Such authorities as exist indicate that claims to enforce adjudicators' awards will be afforded no special privileges. For example, in *Cameron Ltd v John Mowlem & Company plc* 52 BLR 24, the successful party was not entitled to enforce the adjudicator's award either as an arbitration award[9] or in summary proceedings. It was held that the adjudicator's award related only to the entitlement to set-off. It did not establish that the amount claimed was due. The defendant who disputed that the amount claimed was due had a triable defence to the claim and summary judgment was denied. Had the adjudicator been given wider jurisdiction under the contract to ascertain what sum was due, the analysis of the court may well have been different and the award enforced. In contrast, in *Drake & Skull Engineering Ltd v McLaughlin & Harvey plc* 60 BLR 102, a mandatory injunction was granted requiring the defendant to honour the adjudicator's award. In this case, there was no defence outside the adjudicator's jurisdiction and the award was therefore binding. The adjudicator's powers under the Act are more extensive than those granted by the adjudication provisions of many of the standard forms. It is, therefore, likely that defences beyond the adjudicator's jurisdiction available to defeat enforcement of the award will be few.

### 7.2.6 Set-off

Summary judgment will not be given if the defendant is able to raise a triable or arguable defence to the claim. Set-off is a defence to the claim. If the defendant has a set-off he may raise it in the adjudication proceedings. In this case the substantive merits of the set-off will be investigated by the adjudicator. However, it may be in the defendant's interests not to raise a set-off in the adjudication proceedings but to raise it instead in defence to an application to enforce the adjudicator's award in summary proceedings where the substantive merits of the set-off cannot be investigated.[10] In any particular case whether set-off is available against an adjudicator's award will depend upon whether it satisfies the requirements of one of the available classes of set-off.[11]

### 7.2.7   Counterclaim

A counterclaim not amounting to set-off is not a defence. It is a separate claim which for reasons of procedural convenience is permitted to be brought in the same court proceedings as a claim. In the absence of agreement between the parties,[12] a counterclaim not amounting to set-off cannot be raised in the adjudication proceedings commenced for determination of a claim. This is because the counterclaim is a separate dispute which is not the subject of the referral to adjudication. It is not simply a defence to and therefore part of the claim that has been referred to adjudication. Separate adjudication proceedings may be commenced if appropriate for the recovery of the counterclaim. Should the counterclaim be raised in defence to an application to enforce an adjudicator's award, it will not usually prevent judgment—summary or otherwise—upon the award. Often, however, the existence of a counterclaim will justify a stay of execution upon the judgment.[13]

### 7.2.8   Restricting set-off

The parties may by their contract restrict the right to set-off against the adjudicator's award. Set-off would then not be available to resist enforcement. It would also render a stay of execution of the judgment less likely (*Tubeworkers Ltd v Tilbury Construction Ltd* 30 BLR 67).[14] Such a restriction on set-off would not prevent a party from raising a set-off in the adjudication proceedings themselves or pursuing the claim in separate adjudication, court or arbitration proceedings. However, a restriction on the right to set-off against the adjudicator's award may deprive a defendant of his set-off altogether. This is so because if the set-off against the claim raises issues which are not within the jurisdiction of the adjudicator or cannot be advanced within the adjudication timetable, it may not be capable of being referred for decision by the adjudicator and cannot therefore be operative at adjudication stage. If it cannot be operative at enforcement stage either, it can be brought only by way of separate proceedings. The set-off although not the claim upon which the set-off is based is lost. It is suggested that as set-off is a defence to the claim, if raised in the adjudication, the adjudicator can and should take it into account when assessing the validity of the claim whether or not it would be within his jurisdiction if advanced as a separate 'dispute'. This is because an adjudicator cannot properly find that a claim is good if he has failed to look at a defence to it. The defence is an integral part of the claim over which he does have jurisdiction.[15] For reasons appearing in the paragraph *above*, the same does not apply to counterclaims.

### 7.2.9   Referring set-offs and counterclaims to adjudication

The risk of set-offs or counterclaims against adjudicators' awards may be reduced although not removed altogether. The defendant cannot be obliged to raise any set-off or counterclaim he may have in adjudication proceedings. However, there is no reason appearing on the face of s 108 why a claimant should not refer the defendant's set-off or counterclaim to adjudication.[16] Neither party is restricted to referring to adjudication only his own claim—he may refer a 'dispute' whether it arises on his claim or on a cross-claim. In some cases, it will only be the cross-claim about which there is a 'dispute' capable of being referred to adjudication. If the adjudicator finds against the cross-claim, the defendant is bound by that finding and the set-off or counterclaim is not available to resist enforcement proceedings.

## 7.2.10 Arbitration clause

If, in addition to the adjudication provisions of the contract, the parties have agreed an arbitration clause, enforcement of the adjudicator's award must be channelled through the arbitrator.[17] This is because if a contract contains an arbitration clause it is mandatory for a court to grant a stay of court proceedings brought in contravention of the agreement to arbitrate on the application of either party.[18] The court has no discretion to hear the claim and give summary judgment on it[19] and it is probably not open to a court to find that the position of one of the parties is indisputably good or bad such that there is no 'dispute' which may be referred to arbitration (*Hayter v Nelson Home Insurance Co* [1990] 2 Lloyds Rep 265). That enforcement of an adjudicator's award must be through the agreed medium of arbitration is not necessarily a deficiency in the enforcement process. The arbitrator will be subject to the same restraints and have no greater powers than a court to grant or deny giving award in reliance on an adjudicator's award. If the defendant has a defence, it, like any other dispute within the scope of the arbitration clause should properly be referred to arbitration in accordance with the arbitration provisions of the contract. If there is no defence, the arbitrator should enforce the adjudicator's award on the same principles as would a court without reviewing it substantively. Thereafter, enforcement of the arbitrator's award should be reasonably easy by virtue of the procedure set out in s 66 of the Arbitration Act 1996. However, the adjudicator's award may be made, in effect, unenforceable in the short term by an arbitration clause which defers the right to arbitrate until after, say, practical completion of the project. In such a case, enforcement of an adjudicator's award should be excluded from the scope of the arbitration clause.[20]

In order to obtain an arbitrator's award summarily, premised only upon a prior adjudicator's award and without investigation of the substantive merits of the dispute, it is probably not necessary for the arbitrator to have power pursuant to s 39 of the Arbitration Act 1996 to make provisional awards. An arbitration award enforcing an adjudicator's award is, like summary judgment given by a court, final on the issue of the contractual obligation to comply with the adjudicator's award although it is not final as to the underlying merits of the dispute. To avoid any misunderstanding and to put the matter beyond doubt, the parties may wish to confer on the arbitrator power generally or limited to the enforcement of adjudicator's awards to make provisional awards as provided for in s 39 of the Arbitration Act 1996. The parties may further wish to exclude from the scope of the arbitration clause disputes arising in relation to the right to adjudicate or enforcement of adjudication awards. In this event, enforcement can be by direct access to court.[21]

### 7.2.11 Enforcement abroad

The enforcement abroad of court judgments and arbitration awards is available under various international enforcement treaties. None applies to adjudication. If it is necessary to enforce abroad, a party may seek either a court order or an arbitrator's award prior to enforcement. Alternatively, local enforcement procedures may be investigated to ascertain whether any summary procedure is available to give effect to the award as a contractual entitlement.

---

7   An adjudicator's award with interim effect is probably not arbitration. See *A Cameron Ltd v John Mowlem and Co plc* 52 BLR 24.
8   Defences to applications to enforce are dealt with in para **7.5**.
9   The adjudication procedure in that case was not an arbitration.
10  See, however, para **7.2.9**.
11  See *Hanak v Green* [1958] 2 QB 9; *Axel Johnson Petroleum AB v MG Mineral Group AG* [1992] 1 WLR 270; *B Hargreaves Ltd v Action 2000 Ltd* 62 BLR 72; *Dole Dried Fruits and Nut Co v Trustin Kerwood Ltd* [1990] 2 Lloyds Rep 309; *Aectra Refining and Marketing Inc v Exmar NV* [1995] 1 All ER 641. is open to argument that equitable set-off should be denied where the set-off could have been but was not, raised in the adjudication proceedings.
12  Agreement after dispute has arisen may be difficult to obtain. There is no reason why such agreement should not be contained in the construction contract. However, counterclaims will render the adjudication procedure even more hurried than is inevitably the case pursuant to the Act.
13  RSC Ord 14, r 3(2); RSC Ord 47, r 1. This is particularly likely where the defendant was not able to advance his counterclaim in the same proceedings as the claim. See *Schofield v Church Army* [1986] 1 WLR 1329.
14  A stay of execution on judgment may be available where the claimant is insolvent. Whether stay may be granted in these circumstances where set-off is excluded by contract was left open in *Tubeworkers*.
15  If it is only the cross-claim that is in dispute and that is beyond the jurisdiction of the adjudicator, the adjudicator has no jurisdiction over the dispute at all.
16  In many cases defences to claims for payment under the contract will be rendered transparent (such that the claimant knows about them and can refer them to adjudication) by the notice requirements of s 111 of the Act.
17  The insolvency procedures discussed at para **7.2.2** remain available.
18  Section 9(4) of the Arbitration Act 1996.
19  Section 86 of the Arbitration Act 1996 which disapplies s 9(4) to domestic arbitrations has not been brought into effect by the Arbitration Act 1996 (Commencement No 1) Order 1996 (SI No 3146 (C 96)).
20  See cl 66(9) of the April 1998 amendment to ICE 5th and 6th edn and ICE Design and Construct.
21  Particularly important if arbitration under the contract is generally deferred until after completion of the payment.

---

## 7.3   Remedies

A plaintiff for summary judgment may seek any remedy recognised by English law appropriate to his claim. This includes an order for payment of a specific sum of money, an order for damages to be assessed, a declaration, an injunction, specific performance or rectification of the contract. The fact that a party may be entitled to summary judgment does not, in itself, entitle him to any particular remedy. The availability of each remedy must be considered in its own right. In the context of adjudication, when considering the availability of remedies, it should be borne in mind that the adjudication procedure was probably intended to have interim effect only. Those remedies which in fact impose a solution which is permanent and irreversible may for this reason be unavailable to enforce an adjudicator's award.

## .3.1  Money awards

Where the adjudicator has ordered that one party pay a specific sum of money to another the court will usually order the payment of that specific sum of money. If the adjudicator has ordered that a specific sum of money should be paid to a trustee stakeholder or any third party pending final resolution of the dispute, that award can be enforced by a decree of specific performance (*Drake & Skull Engineering Ltd v McLaughlin & Harvey plc* 60 BLR 102). It will be a rare adjudicator's award which orders an unspecified sum of money to be paid, for example, damages to be assessed. There is no reason why a court should not enforce such an award and assess damages itself if the adjudicator does not do so. Such a procedure, however, would not give the parties an effective decision within the time prescribed by the Act.

## .3.2  Non-money awards

The fact that an adjudicator's award is usually intended to have only interim effect pending final resolution of the dispute means that the adjudication procedure will often be inappropriate for the resolution of disputes which do not involve the payment of money. Money can be paid and repaid. Actions cannot be undone. The adjudicator's award in non-money disputes, if acted upon, may result in permanent and irreversible consequences. Some disputes are overtly money disputes. So, a dispute about an alleged entitlement to set off against certified sums for defective work is directly concerned with money. Many disputes which are not on their face about money are in fact indirectly money disputes. So a dispute as to whether an order alleged to constitute a variation pursuant to the contract was in fact authorised by the contract will often be concerned indirectly with money—the matter ultimately of concern to the parties is how the varied works are to be valued, whether in accordance with the contract or on some other basis.

The absence of effective compulsive powers in the adjudicator[22] coupled with the likely reluctance of the courts to exercise their compulsive powers in aid of an adjudicator's award[23] will often mean that there may be limited benefit in advancing in adjudication a dispute whose immediate concern, direct or indirect, is not money, for example, a dispute as to copyright in drawings or the right to assign. The obstacles to enforcing such a non-money award are discussed below.

## .3.3  Specific performance and injunction

The remedies of specific performance and injunction, being creations of equity, are granted, not as of right, but in the discretion of the court. The court will grant these equitable remedies only if the grounds for doing so have been substantiated by the plaintiff. The court has a general jurisdiction to deny them if on the particular facts of any case it is just to do so. It is beyond the scope of this book to analyse in detail the grounds for granting or refusing specific performance o injunction. The following examples illustrate the problems which will face the courts when dealing with applications for specific performance or injunction in reliance upon an adjudicator's award.

Specific performance may be denied if it would cause unfairness to a third party, for example, if it would induce a breach of contract or compel the defend ant to act in a way that he was not lawfully competent to act. So, an adjudicator's award may order a main contractor to assign copyright in drawings to the em ployer in circumstances where the main contractor may be lawfully incompeten so to do for example if copyright is not his to assign. Alternatively, it may cause him to breach his contract with a sub-contractor. A court may be reluctant to grant specific performance in these circumstances.

Specific performance may be refused if it would cause undue hardship to the defendant. For example, an adjudicator may find that a substantial structure whilst safe and serviceable, is not constructed in accordance with the minutiae o the contract and order it to be demolished and rebuilt. Had such case come be fore the court as a claim for damages representing the full cost of rebuilding the structure to the contractual specification, it may have failed (*Ruxley Electronic and Construction v Forsythe* [1996] AC 344). A court is unlikely to grant specific performance.

The equitable remedies of specific performance and injunction will not be or dered where damages are an adequate remedy. In many cases, refusal to comply with a non-money award of the adjudicator will be adequately compensatable in damages. For this reason alone, specific performance and injunction may be re fused. It will usually be the appropriate course of action for a party who obtains in adjudication a non-money award which is not complied with, to seek dam ages for breach of contract. The most convenient forum for such claim will ofter be in another adjudication.

If specific performance or injunction is needed as a remedy, the claimant will often be advised to make application direct to court and not *via* adjudication.

When considering whether an injunction or order for specific performance is appropriate to enforce an adjudicator's award, the likely effect of such an order upon the ability of the parties effectively to reverse the adjudicator's award must be analysed. In *Drake & Skull Engineering Ltd v McLaughlin & Harvey plc* 60 BLF 102, the court drew a distinction between mandatory injunctions which in effec determine the whole of the action and mandatory injunctions of temporary ef fect. As regards the former type of mandatory injunction, it was said that they would be granted only 'in the most extreme circumstances'.[24]

### 7.3.4   Declaration

It will often be inappropriate for a party to seek a declaration in reliance upon an adjudicator's award. This is because if the claim is brought on the adjudicator's award, the only declaration which may be given relates to that award and not to the underlying substantive dispute. So, for example, a court may be persuaded to give a declaration that the adjudicator's award was made, was within the adjudicator's jurisdiction and that the parties are under contractual obligation to comply with it. However, the court will not without investigation of the substantive merits of the dispute, give a declaration on those substantive merits.

### 7.3.5    Rectification

The court will not rectify a contract on the basis of the adjudicator's finding that it should be rectified. This is because rectification would require the court to investigate the substantive merits of the dispute and not simply the fact of an adjudicator's award.

### 7.3.6    Self-help remedies

If a claimant obtains a money award which is not honoured, he may set off the amount of that award against any liability he may incur to the defendant. If an award is not paid, a party may in appropriate circumstances seek to suspend work pursuant to s 112 of the Act. This type of self-help remedy may or may not be available in any particular case and may or may not be advantageous. The Act does not restrict such self-help remedies.

---

22  See para **7.2.1**.
23  See paras **7.3.3**.
24  At p 111.

---

## 7.4    Effect of adjudicator's award

### 7.4.1    Effect of non-compliance

If the adjudicator makes an award, the parties are under a contractual obligation to comply with it (*Drake & Skull Engineering Ltd v McLaughlin & Harvey plc* 60 BLR 102 at p 110; see also s 108(3)). If the parties fail to comply, they are in breach of contract for which damages will be available. The adjudication procedure envisaged by the Act requires that in the absence of agreement to the contrary, the adjudicator's award is binding only until overturned by agreement or in court or arbitration proceedings. It is implicit in this that monies paid under an adjudicator's award subsequently overturned should be repaid.

### 7.4.2    Effect of compliance

A party who is unsuccessful in adjudication may comply with the adjudicator's award and in consequence suffer loss in circumstances where the adjudicator's award is subsequently overturned. For example, in a dispute between an employer and a main contractor, the adjudicator may find that the employer is not entitled to assign the building contract. If the employer honours this decision he may lose the opportunity of a valuable sale. If the adjudicator's award is subsequently overturned in court or arbitration, it is unlikely that the employer can recover from the main contractor the loss of his profit on the sale as he is entitled to no recompense for the costs incurred or losses suffered in complying with his contractual obligations. The contract may, however, provide that each party shall reimburse the other losses flowing from compliance with an adjudicator's award if that award is subsequently overturned in arbitration or in court. Such a provision, whilst acting as a disincentive against pursuing adjudication in these circumstances should not render the contract non-compliant with s 108(3).

## 7.5    Challenge

### 7.5.1    The analogies

The Act makes no provision for challenge to an adjudicator's award. There is little authority upon the circumstances in which an adjudicator's award may be impugned. It is, therefore, necessary to reason by analogy from the grounds of challenge in the contexts of arbitration and expert determination.

### 7.5.2    Error of fact

A court will not entertain a challenge to the adjudicator's award on the basis that the adjudicator has wrongly decided an issue of fact. This is so even if the issue of fact is alleged to be critical to his decision. There would be no point in having an adjudication procedure if the award could be challenged simply on the basis that it is wrong in point of fact.

Even if the adjudicator's award is so wrong in point of fact that no reasonable adjudicator could have reached it, it will still be unchallengeable unless a party is able to sustain an argument that the adjudicator in reaching his decision exceeded his jurisdiction. For example, the adjudicator is required, in the absence of provision to the contrary, to ascertain the parties' substantive rights by applying the appropriate law to the facts of the dispute. If the adjudicator makes a decision which cannot be supported on the material before him, the defendant may be able to raise an argument that the adjudicator did not decide the dispute entrusted to him but some other dispute[25] or that he did not decide it in accordance with the contract but as 'aimable compositeur' which he had no jurisdiction to do. It is only in the most extreme circumstances that such an argument is likely to succeed.

### 7.5.3    Error of law

For the same reasons, a simple error of law will not entitle the defendant to challenge the adjudicator's award. The courts have insisted, in the contexts of arbitration and expert determination, that where the parties have, by their contract, entrusted a decision to a particular person, they must abide by that decision, even if it contains errors of law.

### 7.5.4    Errors of law going to the adjudicator's jurisdiction

In *Jones v Sherwood Computer Services plc* [1992] 1 WLR 277, it was said by the Court of Appeal that an expert determination, stated by the contract to be 'final, conclusive and binding for all purposes' was precisely that, and that a mistake of law would not entitle one of the parties to challenge the determination. The exception to this principle is if the expert departed from his instructions in a material respect. For example, in that case which concerned the valuation of shares, if the expert had valued the wrong number of shares or had valued shares in the wrong company or if the expert had valued machinery himself whereas his instructions were to employ an expert valuer of his choice, either party would be entitled to challenge the expert determination because the expert had not done what he was appointed to do.[26] In other words, he would have acted in excess of jurisdiction.

This decision has been applied and approved on a number of occasions. In *Nikko Hotels (UK) Ltd v MEPC plc* (1991) 28 EG 86 it was said by Knox J that if parties agree to refer to the final and conclusive judgment of an expert an issue which either consists of a question of construction or necessarily involves the solution of a question of construction, the expert's decision will be final and conclusive. It will not be open to review or treatment by the courts as a nullity on the ground that the expert's decision on construction was erroneous in law unless it can be shown that the expert has not performed the task assigned to him. If he has answered the right question in the wrong way, his decision will be binding. If he has answered the wrong question, his decision will be a nullity (*Nikko Hotels (UK) Ltd v MEPC plc* [1991] 2 EGLR 103 at p 108).

### 7.5.5   Analogy with expert determination

The authorities cited above involved contracts providing that the expert determination should be final and conclusive. Most adjudication agreements will provide that the award is to be binding only until the dispute is finally resolved elsewhere. However, it is suggested that the above analysis in the expert determination cases is appropriate in the adjudication context. Not only is it an analysis which gives effect to the adjudication procedure but it is also an analysis which recognises the contractual status of the adjudicator's award. The courts should not interfere, on an interim basis, with an adjudicator's award on the grounds of error of law or fact any more than they interfere with the final determination of an expert given under a contract providing that the expert determination is of final and conclusive effect.

However, it is not suggested that the analogy between expert determination and adjudication is perfect. In particular, expert determination providing a final and conclusive outcome to an issue or a dispute will have a more permanent and definitive effect upon the parties' substantive rights than an adjudicator's award which is of temporary effect only. For this reason, care should be taken when reasoning by analogy with authorities in the context of expert determination which resile from the robust approach taken in *Jones v Sherwood* and *Nikko Hotels* (*above*).

### 7.5.6   Jurisdiction

If the adjudicator acts in excess of his jurisdiction in any respect his award will be a nullity. This is clear from *Jones v Sherwood* and *Nikko Hotels (UK) Ltd v MEPC Plc* (*above*). The authority of an adjudicator's award stems from the contract granting him jurisdiction. If he disregards the limits of the powers granted to him for example, by conducting the adjudication in a manner which does not accord with the powers conferred on him by his terms of appointment or, where appropriate, the underlying construction contract, he may be acting in excess of jurisdiction. If the adjudicator has made a decision beyond the authority granted by that contract, it can be of no effect. Excess of jurisdiction can be blatant and obvious, such as, for example, if a person, purporting to act as adjudicator, decides a dispute which neither party has referred to him. Alternatively, excess of jurisdiction may be subtle and ascertainable only following protracted debate. In either case, the adjudicator's award will not be enforceable. The ways in which an adjudicator may exceed his jurisdiction are far too numerous to list. In most cases, excess of jurisdiction will imply no improper conduct on the part of the adjudicator. It was seen in Chapter 3 that s 108 of the Act is drafted in such a way as to facilitate jurisdictional challenge and there is no statutory restriction upon when such challenge may be made.[27]

### 7.5.7   Procedural unfairness

It has been said (*London Export Corporation v Jubilee Coffee Roasting Company* [1958] 1 Lloyds Rep 197) in the context of arbitration that 'an award obtained in violation of the rules of natural justice even where there is no breach of the agreed procedure would be set aside on grounds of public policy'. In *R v Disciplinary Committee of the Jockey Club, ex p Aga Khan* [1993] 1 WLR 909 *per* Hoffmann LJ it was said that in that case:

> 'the remedies in private law available to the Aga Khan seem ... entirely adequate. He has a contract with the Jockey Club ... The Club has an implied obligation under the contract to conduct its disciplinary proceedings fairly. If it has not done so, the Aga Khan can obtain a declaration that the decision was ineffective ... and, if necessary, an injunction to restrain the Jockey Club from doing anything to implement it.'

It is likely that the courts will take a similar view to procedural unfairness in adjudication.[28] As the content of the duty of procedural fairness is not free from doubt[29] allegations of procedural unfairness, including failure to act with impartiality, may provide a fertile ground for dispute as to the effectiveness and enforceability of adjudicators' awards.

### 7.5.8   Bad faith

If it can be shown that the adjudicator acted fraudulently or in collusion with one of the parties, his award will almost certainly not be enforced. Nor will it be enforced where it can be shown to have been obtained by fraud of one of the parties. It would be against public policy for a court to be seen to lend assistance to the enforcement of an adjudicator's award obtained in these circumstances. If the adjudicator has acted in bad faith, he is not required by s 108(4) to be immune from suit of the parties. Any general immunity from suit conferred upon the adjudicator by the contract, will not, in the absence of very express words, cover fraud.

### 7.5.9 Challenge before award—by agreement

The parties are free to agree to seek a court ruling upon the proper interpretation of their contract. If they do so, the ruling obtained, if it is not sufficient to resolve the dispute, should be used as a guide by the adjudicator in doing so.

### 7.5.10 Challenge before award—unilateral

In the context of adjudication, unilateral challenge before award will usually not be possible. The adjudicator has 28 days, extendible to no more than 42 days unless both parties consent, to reach his decision. It will be rare that an application to court which is disputed will be resolved before the award is delivered. A court has no power to suspend the adjudication procedure to allow a court ruling to be made at the instigation of one party unilaterally.[30]

In *Postel Properties Ltd v Greenwell* [1992] EGLR 130, the court rejected the contention that because the court will not upset a determination once made, therefore it should not make a ruling on a point relevant to a determination yet to be made. However, in *Norwich Union Life Insurance Society v P&O Property Holdings Ltd* [1993] 1 EGLR 164, the Court of Appeal decided that if the question upon which the ruling was sought was within the jurisdiction of the expert the court should not substitute its determination for that of the expert before or after award. The application for an interlocutory injunction in that case was denied.

If adjudication were a mandatory and conclusive procedure it is likely that no unilateral application for a court ruling on a matter within the adjudicator's jurisdiction would be entertained. This is because it is the adjudicator and not the court who is entrusted with the role of making the decision. However, adjudication under s 108 of the Act is not a mandatory procedure, nor is it a binding procedure. The parties can refer a dispute to adjudication if they wish but are not obliged to do so. They are not finally bound by the decision if they do. The adjudicator does not have sole jurisdiction. In these circumstances, it cannot be said that it is the adjudicator's and not the court's determination that should prevail. A court or arbitration ruling may, therefore, be entertained in appropriate circumstances.

---

25  See the reasoning in *Jones v Sherwood* [1992] 1 WLR 277 and *Nikko Hotels (UK) Ltd v MEPC plc* (1991) 28 EG 86, discussed at paras **7.5.4–7.5.6**. The same reasoning should apply equally to mistakes of fact.
26  Page 287.
27  There is no equivalent in the context of adjudication of s 31 of the Arbitration Act 1996 which restricts the time in which challenges to the arbitration's jurisdiction may be made.
28  There may be a lower threshold of what is procedural unfairness in the context of adjudication. See Chapter 4.
29  See paras **4.3.1–4.3.7**
30  In *Postel Properties Ltd v Greenwell* [1992] EGLR 130, a concession that the expert determination process could not be suspended pending the court's ruling was accepted.

## 7.6     Reversal proceedings

### 7.6.1   No statutory limitations

There is no limit within the Act upon the time within which reversal proceedings may be commenced. There is no requirement that proceedings be commenced for the specific purpose of overturning the adjudicator's award. Proceedings many years after the award may have the effect of overturning the award even if commenced for an entirely distinct reason. For example, if an adjudicator finds that a design and build contractor's designs meet the contractual specification such as to disentitle the employer from setting off against sums otherwise due to the contractor, the employer may nevertheless seek an indemnity or contribution from the contractor at some later date if defects in those designs cause loss to a third party to whom the employer is responsible. It is within the power of the parties to limit by their contract the time within which reversal proceedings must be commenced. It is further within their power to agree that the adjudication award is to be finally determinative of their rights.[31]

### 7.6.2   Effect of reversal

If an adjudicator's award for the payment of money is honoured but subsequently overturned the paying party will seek recovery of sums paid pursuant to the award. It is implicit in a contract providing for a dispute resolution procedure the result of which may be reversed in court or arbitration that money paid over under the procedure reversed should be repaid. If there were no such implied term, the parties may in some instances find themselves in the unsatisfactory position of relying upon a restitutionary remedy for the recovery of money paid.

The parties may wish to put the matter beyond argument by making provision for repayment in such circumstances and/or provision whereby they indemnify each other against losses incurred in compliance with the adjudicator's award if it is subsequently overturned. Such indemnity would not necessarily extend to the costs expended or ordered to be paid in the adjudication. Such costs cannot be said to have been incurred in compliance with the adjudicator's award. If it is sought to recover these costs, express provision should be made in the contract.

If a non money award, which is dishonoured, is compensated by a money award for breach of contract, the reversal of the first non money award will not necessarily imply repayment of sums paid under the subsequent money award for breach of contract. In fact (see *above* for reasons) parties to an adjudication have no justification for refusing to comply with an award simply because it is wrong. If this analysis is correct, a party which becomes liable for damages for failure to comply with an award which is subsequently overturned, cannot expect that liability to be reversed simply because the award on the underlying merits of the dispute (which has interim binding effect on the parties) has been reversed. Express contractual provision is required if this result is to be achieved.

### 7.6.3   Nature of reversal proceedings

The adjudicator's award may be overturned in court or arbitration proceedings by the successful party seeking to increase the quantum of his award or by the unsuccessful party seeking to reduce or eliminate his liability. Any proceedings in court or arbitration between the parties to the award may result in the award being reversed. In the absence of express contractual provision to the contrary, reversal proceedings will be a complete re-hearing of the dispute—they will not be an appeal. The parties are, however, free to restrict the reversal proceedings as they see fit. For example, the contract may provide that the reversal proceedings be limited to reviewing the adjudicator's award in point of law. Or, the contract may restrict the evidence and argument at the re-hearing procedure to that brought in the adjudication proceedings. In circumstances where the adjudicator's award will usually have been made in some haste, without access to all potentially relevant material and where it may not be a reasoned award, the parties will usually wish to reserve their right to a complete re-hearing of the dispute.

---

31  It is not clear from the express wording of s 108(3) whether the right to 'accept the decision … as finally determining their dispute' refers to 'acceptance' only after the award or in the underlying construction contract. The use of the word 'accept' suggests that the agreement to be finally bound by the award must be made after the award is given. However, if this were to be the case, there would be no need for s 108(3) at all as there can be little doubt that the parties are entitled by contract after award to compromise the dispute whether on the terms found by the adjudicator or on any other terms. It does not require statutory provision to achieve this effect. Furthermore, the intention of the Act was to assist in the resolution of disputes and to enable disputes to be resolved quickly and cheaply. It was not intended to proscribe any particular agreed mechanism for doing so. For these reasons, it is suggested that agreement in the construction contract that the award will finally determine the dispute is not inconsistent with the Act but is expressly permitted by s 108(3).

# Epilogue

---

## Introduction

The Latham Report subjected the construction industry to serious criticism. Poor cash flow and claims oriented attitudes were singled out for particular mention. Adjudication appeared the panacea. For a while, criticism of the Latham Report was politically unacceptable. Had it been more openly debated immediately after issue, many of the difficulties with adjudication which have now come to light may have been avoided. The Latham Report itself was concerned with an industry and not with the law governing it. Translating the ideals of the Latham Report into workable legislation has not proved easy.

It is not the purpose of this book to applaud or criticise the objectives intended to be achieved by the Act. It is, however, clear that the adjudication provisions of the Act will raise a large number of questions to which there is no answer in the Act and no satisfactory answer to be found in the general law. The minimalist approach to legislation adopted in the Act is likely to cause uncertainty and confusion as to the meaning and effect of the statutory requirements. Moreover, the Act is silent on many crucial issues, such as, for example, it does not address at all the question of enforcing adjudicator's awards and appears to overlook the difficulties of treating an adjudicator's award as nothing more than a temporary contractual right. The relatively novel concept of inquisitorial proceedings in England is not supported by any useful guidance. In short, the operation of the Act in the context of pre-existing laws does not appear to have been considered at all.

## Unrealistic timetable

The statutory timetable for adjudication set out in s 108 is unrealistically short. It makes no allowance for the complex nature of disputes that arise in the construction industry, the voluminous documentation generated or the mobility of the workforce. Most significantly, it makes no concession to the fact that if the industry is required to invest considerable effort into a high pressure, fast track dispute resolution procedure it will inevitably distract effort from the industry' predominant function of construction.

Adjudication as provided for in the Act is open to abuse. The spectre of a defendant rushed into defending a claim in a period of less than 28 days when the claimant has prepared his case at leisure is not difficult to foresee. A group of claimants acting in consort, by commencing adjudication against the same defendant at the same time, may maximise the pressure applied to the defendant and minimise the defendant's prospects of fairly defending the claims. A tactically timed adjudication application may catch the defendant at a time when he is unable properly to defend a claim. The blackmail potential of adjudication must not be underestimated. The adjudicator is probably not entitled to take into account the behaviour of the parties when rendering his decision—he must apply the law of the contract to the facts of the dispute. It is not for the adjudicator to pass judgment on the exercise by the parties of rights expressly conferred by statute. It is to be hoped that the construction industry acts responsibly in the exercise of the right to adjudication provided by the Act. If it does not, the statutory right to adjudication will quickly fall into disrepute.

## Insurance

Construction insurance contracts are not within the scope of the Act. However, the contracts under which insured liability arises will often be subject to the statutory right to adjudication. From the perspective of the insured, the necessity to conduct the procedure within 28 days and the risk of ambush are serious. However, if (but only if) the liability of insurers arises on the issue of an adverse adjudicator's award, the insured's position is at least protected. Insurers, however, are in an invidious position. If they are to take part in the defence of their insured they will have some period less than 28 days within which to assess liability to provide cover or proceed to defend with all rights reserved, take all necessary steps to ascertain detail about the case and defend. Thereafter they may be limited to seven days for payment of any adverse award.[1] A liability which is subject to reinsurance will give rise to even greater logistical difficulties.

## Role of the professionals

Concern has been expressed that the role of the adjudicator undermines the role of independent arbiter intended to be played by professionals engaged under many standard and bespoke forms of contract. It is often the architect or the engineer who, acting impartially, is charged with determining disputed issues between the parties, such as, for example, extensions of time. The professional's role often goes much further than this and he will often act as the primary and secondary method of resolving disputes.[2] An adjudicator's decision, taken in a state of relative ignorance, may, if it casts doubt upon a prior decision of such a professional, result in mistrust, misunderstanding and loss of confidence in the relationships between the various parties to construction projects.

If adjudicators have power to review certificates, the professionals issuing those certificates may find their relationship with their clients become more difficult to maintain. Any loss of confidence by the client in his professional advisers would be an unwelcome development in the construction industry. It would be all the more regrettable if the loss of confidence was brought about by nothing more than an adjudicator's award overturning, on familiarity with the project extending to no more than 28 days, the certificate of a professional who may have been intimately acquainted with the project from its inception. In strict legal terms, an adjudicator's award between a client and the contractor has no impact upon the professional. In practical terms, however, many professionals, under increasing pressure on their fees, may find in such circumstances that an adjudicator's award is used to tactical advantage by the client in an endeavour to reduce fees still further.

There is no reason why one of the professionals engaged upon the project should not be appointed adjudicator. However, this will often be an unattractive option—many within the industry are sceptical about the professional's ability to act impartially in circumstances where his own contractual performance to his client may be brought into question. Many more doubt whether it is realistic to ask a professional to change a decision which he has already made, not by means of the remeasurement or review procedures of the contract, but through the dispute resolution mechanisms. In these circumstances, a truly independent and impartial review may be of benefit to the industry. It is not, however, realistic to expect the parties to be satisfied with the approximate and necessarily peremptory approach that an adjudicator is able to take to the potentially very complex issues involved in the time available to him under the Act. A cynic might say that the only party likely to be satisfied with such an approach is the winner.

## Assumption of solvency

The Act sets apart the construction industry from the rest of the business world. The construction industry is obliged to accept certain statutory requirements and restrictions, not simply those relating to adjudication.[3] Those restrictions and requirements apply to no other person, partnership or company in the entire country.

What has been described as the 'pay now, argue later' culture assumes continued solvency on the part of the recipient of a money award, such that he will be able to repay later if necessary. This is an assumption which may not be justified on the recent financial history of the industry. Whatever the merits of the ideology of the Act, it is difficult to escape the conclusion that, as a piece of legislation, it was enacted in haste and without sufficient analysis of its likely operation in practice. It is, therefore, necessary to fill gaps left in the structure of the adjudication procedure by arguing by analogy with other dispute resolution procedures and by reference to the common law in general. It is only when a sufficient body of case law on adjudication has developed that a truly authoritative statement of the law of adjudication can be made. In the meantime, it is hoped that readers will find the views expressed and analogies drawn in this book of assistance in drafting, operating, enforcing and litigating over adjudication procedures. It is further hoped that they will be lenient in judgment of the author's errors.

---

1   See s 111(4).
2   See, for example, FIDIC 4th Ed, clause 67.
3   For example, s 111 restricts the right of set off.

# Appendix A
# Checklist

*When drafting adjudication agreements consider the following.*

## DOES THE ACT APPLY?

| No | Issue | Para ref |
|----|-------|----------|
| 1 | Is there a contract? | 2.7.5 |
| 2 | Is it in writing? | 2.7 |
| 3 | Is the contract concluded at a time when it is subject to the Act? | 2.2.2 |
| 4 | Is it a construction contract? | 2.3 |
| | Contract for works | 2.3.1 |
| | Procuring works | 2.3.5 |
| | Labour | 2.3.6 |
| | Professional services | 2.3.7, 2.3.8 |
| | Employment contracts | 2.3.9 |
| | Bonds/guarantees | 2.3.3, 2.8.3 |
| | Insurance | 2.3.4, 2.8.3 |
| | Collateral warranties | 2.3.2 |
| | Financing contracts | 2.3.10, 2.8.3 |
| 5 | Does the contract relate to construction operations? | 2.4 |
| 6 | Is the contract excluded? | 2.5, 2.8 |
| 7 | Is it an excluded contract with a residential occupier? | 2.6.1 |
| 8 | Is the adjudication provision in writing? | 2.7 |
| 9 | Is the contract within the territorial jurisdiction of the Act? | 2.2.1 |
| 10 | Is the Act applicable to part only of the contract? | 2.2.3 |

## SCOPE OF ADJUDICATION AGREEMENT

| 11 | Is agreement properly characterised as adjudication or some other procedure? | 1.3.3 |
|----|-------|----------|
| 12 | Is adjudication to be an obligation or a right? | 3.3.2 |

| No | Issue | Para ref |
|----|-------|----------|
| 13 | Is adjudication a condition precedent to other dispute resolution procedures? | 3.1.3 |
| 14 | Are proceedings to reverse the adjudicator's award (or indeed any other proceedings) to be deferred until after completion of the works? | 3.1.3, 7.2.10 |
| 15 | Is adjudication to be an interim procedure or finally determinative of the parties' rights? | 4.6, 7.6.3 |
| 16 | What forum will finally determine the dispute—court, arbitration or other? | 3.4.9 |

## THE ADJUDICATOR

| | | |
|----|-------|----------|
| 17 | Sole adjudicator or panel? | 5.2.2 |
| 18 | Is adjudicator to be appointed at outset of project or only when a dispute arises? | 5.2.2 |
| 19 | How is he to be appointed? | 3.3.3, 4.2.11 |
| 20 | Is he required to have particular qualifications or expertise? | 5.2.2 |
| 21 | Contract with adjudicator. | 5.1.3, 5.2.1 |
| 22 | Who pays the adjudicator's fees in the first instance and how much are they to be? | 5.2.4–5.2.9 |
| 23 | What expenses is the adjudicator allowed? | 5.2.8 |
| 24 | How are adjudicator's fees to be ascertained in the event of disagreement with the parties? | 5.2.5 |
| 25 | Can the adjudicator's fees be recovered by one party from the other following the outcome of the adjudication? | 5.2.6 |
| 26 | Is the adjudicator to be paid in advance/on account or be entitled to exercise a lien for his fees? | 5.2.10 |

## THE ADJUDICATOR'S POWERS, RIGHTS AND DUTIES

| | | |
|----|-------|----------|
| 27 | Do the parties require the adjudicator to have power to review certificates? Does the adjudicator need such power to be expressly conferred upon him? Does the contract confer it? | 3.4.6–3.4.9 |
| 28 | If so, is power validly conferred upon the tribunal with authority finally to resolve the dispute to do likewise and overturn the adjudicator's award? | 3.4.9 |
| 29 | Is the adjudicator to have power to act as 'aimable compositeur' or make a decision on some basis other than the parties legal | |

| No | Issue | Para ref |
|----|-------|----------|
| | entitlements?  If so, what basis? | 4.2.17 |
| 30 | Is the adjudicator to have power to make interlocutory orders? | 5.4.1 |
| 31 | May the adjudicator order the payment of interest? | |
| | If so, how assessed? | 5.4.2 |
| 32 | May the adjudicator make an order for the payment of costs? | |
| | If so, calculated on what basis? | |
| | How are they to be taxed? | 5.4.3 |
| 33 | Adjudicator under obligation to act impartially. | 4.3 |
| 34 | Must the adjudicator be impartial? | 4.3.6 |
| 35 | Adjudicator to have power to take the initiative in ascertaining fact | |
| | and law. | 4.4 |
| 36 | The adjudicator is to be immune from suit. | 4.5 |
| 37 | Is the adjudicator to have authority to appoint technical and/or | |
| | legal advisers and recover the costs of so doing from the parties? | 4.4.3 |

## THE DISPUTE

| No | Issue | Para ref |
|----|-------|----------|
| 38 | Any dispute must be capable of being referred to adjudication. | 3.4.11, |
| | There must be no restriction on disputes referable or the time | 3.4.12, 4.2.7 |
| | when they may be referred. | |
| 39 | Do the parties wish to agree a procedure for crystallising disputes? | 3.4.5 |
| 40 | Disputes arising 'under' the contract must be referable.  Should | |
| | other disputes be referable, such as disputes arising 'out of', 'in | |
| | respect of' or 'in connection with' the contract? | 3.5 |

## THE PROCEDURE

| No | Issue | Para ref |
|----|-------|----------|
| 41 | There must be an entitlement in all parties to serve notice of | |
| | intention to refer a dispute to adjudication at any time. | 4.2.4 |
| 42 | Form of notice. | 4.2.5 |
| 43 | Content of notice. | 4.2.6 |
| 44 | Time of notice. | 4.2.7 |
| 45 | Timetable for appointment of adjudicator and referral of dispute | |
| | must comply with the Act. | 4.2.8, 4.2.9, |
| | | 4.2.12 |
| 46 | Are there to be express procedural requirements of referral? | 4.2.12 |
| 47 | Time for adjudicator to reach his decision must comply with the Act. | 4.2.14 |
| 48 | Extensions of time? | 4.2.15 |

# Appendix B

# Part II of the Housing Grants, Construction and Regeneration Act 1996

*Introductory provisions*

**104.**—(1) In this Part a "construction contract" means an agreement with a person for any of the following—

    (a)    the carrying out of construction operations;

    (b)    arranging for the carrying out of construction operations by others, whether under sub-contract to him or otherwise;

    (c)    providing his own labour, or the labour of others, for the carrying out of construction operations.

  (2)  References in this Part to a construction contract include an agreement—

    (a)    to do architectural, design, or surveying work, or

    (b)    to provide advice on building, engineering, interior or exterior decoration or on the laying-out of landscape,

in relation to construction operations.

  (3)  References in this Part to a construction contract do not include a contract of employment (within the meaning of the Employment Rights Act 1996).

  (4)  The Secretary of State may by order add to, amend or repeal any of the provisions of subsection (1), (2) or (3) as to the agreements which are construction contracts for the purposes of this Part or are to be taken or not to be taken as included in references to such contracts.

No such order shall be made unless a draft of it has been laid before and approved by a resolution of each House of Parliament.

  (5)  Where an agreement relates to construction operations and other matters, this Part applies to it only so far as it relates to construction operations.

An agreement relates to construction operations so far as it makes provision of any kind within subsection (1) or (2).

  (6)  This Part applies only to construction contracts which—

    (a)    are entered into after the commencement of this Part, and

    (b)    relate to the carrying out of construction operations in England, Wales or Scotland.

  (7)  This Part applies whether or not the law of England and Wales or Scotland is otherwise the applicable law in relation to the contract.

Construction contracts.

1996 c.18.

**105.**—(1) In this Part "construction operations" means, subject as follows, operations o any of the following descriptions—

(a) construction, alteration, repair, maintenance, extension, demolition or dis mantling of buildings, or structures forming, or to form, part of the land (whether permanent or not);

(b) construction, alteration, repair, maintenance, extension, demolition or dis mantling of any works forming, or to form, part of the land, including (without prejudice to the foregoing) walls, roadworks, power-lines, telecom munication apparatus, aircraft runways, docks and harbours, railways inland waterways, pipe-lines, reservoirs, water-mains, wells, sewers, indus trial plant and installations for purposes of land drainage, coast protection o defence;

(c) installation in any building or structure of fittings forming part of the land including (without prejudice to the foregoing) systems of heating, lighting air-conditioning, ventilation, power supply, drainage, sanitation, water supply or fire protection, or security or communications systems;

(d) external or internal cleaning of buildings and structures, so far as carried ou in the course of their construction, alteration, repair, extension or restoration

(e) operations which form an integral part of, or are preparatory to, or are fo rendering complete, such operations as are previously described in this subsection, including site clearance, earth-moving, excavation, tunnelling and boring, laying of foundations, erection, maintenance or dismantling o scaffolding, site restoration, landscaping and the provision of roadways and other access works;

(f) painting or decorating the internal or external surfaces of any building o structure.

(2) The following operations are not construction operations within the meaning o this Part—

(a) drilling for, or extraction of, oil or natural gas;

(b) extraction (whether by underground or surface working) of minerals; tun nelling or boring, or construction of underground works, for this purpose;

(c) assembly, installation or demolition of plant or machinery, or erection o demolition of steelwork for the purposes of supporting or providing access to plant or machinery, on a site where the primary activity is—

   (i) nuclear processing, power generation, or water or effluent treatment, or

   (ii) the production, transmission, processing or bulk storage (other than warehousing) of chemicals, pharmaceuticals, oil, gas, steel or food and drink;

(d) manufacture or delivery to site of—

   (i) building or engineering components or equipment,

   (ii) materials, plant or machinery, or

   (iii) components for systems of heating, lighting, air-conditioning, ventila tion, power supply, drainage, sanitation, water supply or fire protec tion, or for security or communications systems, except under a contract which also provides for their installation;

(e) the making, installation and repair of artistic works, being sculptures, murals and other works which are wholly artistic in nature.

(3) The Secretary of State may by order add to, amend or repeal any of the provisions o subsection (1) or (2) as to the operations and work to be treated as construction operations for the purposes of this Part.

(4) No such order shall be made unless a draft of it has been laid before and approved by a resolution of each House of Parliament.

**106.**—(1) This Part does not apply—

Part II
Provisions not
applicable to
contract with
residential
occupier.

(a)    to a construction contract with a residential occupier (see below), or

(b)    to any other description of construction contract excluded from the operation of this Part by order of the Secretary of State.

(2)    A construction contract with a residential occupier means a construction contract which principally relates to operations on a dwelling which one of the parties to the contract occupies, or intends to occupy, as his residence.

In this subsection "dwelling" means a dwelling-house or a flat; and for this purpose—

"dwelling-house" does not include a building containing a flat; and

"flat" means separate and self-contained premises constructed or adapted for use for residential purposes and forming part of a building from some other part of which the premises are divided horizontally.

(3)    The Secretary of State may by order amend subsection (2).

(4)    No order under this section shall be made unless a draft of it has been laid before and approved by a resolution of each House of Parliament.

**107.**—(1) The provisions of this Part apply only where the construction contract is in writing, and any other agreement between the parties as to any matter is effective for the purposes of this Part only if in writing.

The expressions "agreement", "agree" and "agreed" shall be construed accordingly.

(2)    There is an agreement in writing—

(a)    if the agreement is made in writing (whether or not it is signed by the parties),

(b)    if the agreement is made by exchange of communications in writing, or

(c)    if the agreement is evidenced in writing.

(3)    Where parties agree otherwise than in writing by reference to terms which are in writing, they make an agreement in writing.

(4)    An agreement is evidenced in writing if an agreement made otherwise than in writing is recorded by one of the parties, or by a third party, with the authority of the parties to the agreement.

(5)    An exchange of written submissions in adjudication proceedings, or in arbitral or legal proceedings in which the existence of an agreement otherwise than in writing is alleged by one party against another party and not denied by the other party in his response constitutes as between those parties an agreement in writing to the effect alleged.

(6)    References in this Part to anything being written or in writing include its being recorded by any means.

*Adjudication*

**108.**—(1) A party to a construction contract has the right to refer a dispute arising under the contract for adjudication under a procedure complying with this section.

For this purpose "dispute" includes any difference.

(2)    The contract shall—

(a)    enable a party to give notice at any time of his intention to refer a dispute to adjudication;

(b)    provide a timetable with the object of securing the appointment of the adjudicator and referral of the dispute to him within 7 days of such notice;

(c)    require the adjudicator to reach a decision within 28 days of referral or such longer period as is agreed by the parties after the dispute has been referred;

(d)    allow the adjudicator to extend the period of 28 days by up to 14 days, with the consent of the party by whom the dispute was referred;

(e)    impose a duty on the adjudicator to act impartially; and

(f)    enable the adjudicator to take the initiative in ascertaining the facts and the law.

(3)    The contract shall provide that the decision of the adjudicator is binding until the

PART II

dispute is finally determined by legal proceedings, by arbitration (if the contract provides for arbitration or the parties otherwise agree to arbitration) or by agreement.

The parties may agree to accept the decision of the adjudicator as finally determining the dispute.

(4)   The contract shall also provide that the adjudicator is not liable for anything done or omitted in the discharge or purported discharge of his functions as adjudicator unless the act or omission is in bad faith, and that any employee or agent of the adjudicator is similarly protected from liability.

(5)   If the contract does not comply with the requirements of subsections (1) to (4), the adjudication provisions of the Scheme for Construction Contracts apply.

1996 c.23.

(6)   For England and Wales, the Scheme may apply the provisions of the Arbitration Act 1996 with such adaptations and modifications as appear to the Minister making the scheme to be appropriate.

For Scotland, the Scheme may include provision conferring powers on courts in relation to adjudication and provision relating to the enforcement of the adjudicator's decision.

*Payment*

Entitlement to stage payments.

**109.**—(1) A party to a construction contract is entitled to payment by instalments, stage payments or other periodic payments for any work under the contract unless—

(a)   it is specified in the contract that the duration of the work is to be less than 45 days, or

(b)   it is agreed between the parties that the duration of the work is estimated to be less than 45 days.

(2)   The parties are free to agree the amounts of the payments and the intervals at which, or circumstances in which, they become due.

(3)   In the absence of such agreement, the relevant provisions of the Scheme for Construction Contracts apply.

(4)   References in the following sections to a payment under the contract include a payment by virtue of this section.

Dates for payment.

**110.**—(1) Every construction contract shall—

(a)   provide an adequate mechanism for determining what payments become due under the contract, and when, and

(b)   provide for a final date for payment in relation to any sum which becomes due.

The parties are free to agree how long the period is to be between the date on which a sum becomes due and the final date for payment.

(2)   Every construction contract shall provide for the giving of notice by a party not later than five days after the date on which a payment becomes due from him under the contract, or would have become due if—

(a)   the other party had carried out his obligations under the contract, and

(b)   no set-off or abatement was permitted by reference to any sum claimed to be due under one or more other contracts,

specifying the amount (if any) of the payment made or proposed to be made, and the basis on which that amount was calculated.

(3)   If or to the extent that a contract does not contain such provision as is mentioned in subsection (1) or (2), the relevant provisions of the Scheme for Construction Contracts apply.

Notice of intention to withhold payment.

**111.**—(1) A party to a construction contract may not withhold payment after the final date for payment of a sum due under the contract unless he has given an effective notice of intention to withhold payment.

The notice mentioned in section 110(2) may suffice as a notice of intention to withhold payment if it complies with the requirements of this section.

(2)   To be effective such a notice must specify—

(a)   the amount proposed to be withheld and the ground for withholding payment, or

(b)   if there is more than one ground, each ground and the amount attributable to it,

and must be given not later than the prescribed period before the final date for payment.

(3)   The parties are free to agree what that prescribed period is to be.

In the absence of such agreement, the period shall be that provided by the Scheme for Construction Contracts.

(4)   Where an effective notice of intention to withhold payment is given, but on the matter being referred to adjudication it is decided that the whole or part of the amount should be paid, the decision shall be construed as requiring payment not later than—

(a)   seven days from the date of the decision, or

(b)   the date which apart from the notice would have been the final date for payment,

whichever is the later.

112.—(1) Where a sum due under a construction contract is not paid in full by the final date for payment and no effective notice to withhold payment has been given, the person to whom the sum is due has the right (without prejudice to any other right or remedy) to suspend performance of his obligations under the contract to the party by whom payment ought to have been made ("the party in default").

Right to suspend performance for non-payment.

(2)   The right may not be exercised without first giving to the party in default at least seven days' notice of intention to suspend performance, stating the ground or grounds on which it is intended to suspend performance.

(3)   The right to suspend performance ceases when the party in default makes payment in full of the amount due.

(4)   Any period during which performance is suspended in pursuance of the right conferred by this section shall be disregarded in computing for the purposes of any contractual time limit the time taken, by the party exercising the right or by a third party, to complete any work directly or indirectly affected by the exercise of the right.

Where the contractual time limit is set by reference to a date rather than a period, the date shall be adjusted accordingly.

113.—(1) A provision making payment under a construction contract conditional on the payer receiving payment from a third person is ineffective, unless that third person, or any other person payment by whom is under the contract (directly or indirectly) a condition of payment by that third person, is insolvent.

Prohibition of conditional payment provisions.

(2)   For the purposes of this section a company becomes insolvent—

(a)   on the making of an administration order against it under Part II of the Insolvency Act 1986,

1986 c.45.

(b)   on the appointment of an administrative receiver or a receiver or manager of its property under Chapter I of Part III of that Act, or the appointment of a receiver under Chapter II of that Part,

(c)   on the passing of a resolution for voluntary winding-up without a declaration of solvency under section 89 of that Act, or

(d)   on the making of a winding-up order under Part IV or V of that Act.

(3)   For the purposes of this section a partnership becomes insolvent—

(a)   on the making of a winding-up order against it under any provision of the Insolvency Act 1986 as applied by an order under section 420 of that Act, or

(b)   when sequestration is awarded on the estate of the partnership under section 12 of the Bankruptcy (Scotland) Act 1985 or the partnership grants a trust deed for its creditors.

1985 c.66.

(4)   For the purposes of this section an individual becomes insolvent—

(a)   on the making of a bankruptcy order against him under Part IX of the Insolvency Act 1986, or

1986 c.45.

(b)   on the sequestration of his estate under the Bankruptcy (Scotland) Act 1985 or when he grants a trust deed for his creditors.

(5) A company, partnership or individual shall also be treated as insolvent on the occurrence of any event corresponding to those specified in subsection (2), (3) or (4) under the law of Northern Ireland or of a country outside the United Kingdom.

(6) Where a provision is rendered ineffective by subsection (1), the parties are free to agree other terms for payment.

In the absence of such agreement, the relevant provisions of the Scheme for Construction Contracts apply.

*Supplementary provisions*

The Scheme for Construction contracts.

**114.**—(1) The Minister shall by regulations make a scheme ("the Scheme for Construction Contracts ") containing provision about the matters referred to in the preceding provisions of this Part.

(2) Before making any regulations under this section the Minister shall consult such persons as he thinks fit.

(3) In this section "the Minister" means—

(a) for England and Wales, the Secretary of State, and

(b) for Scotland, the Lord Advocate.

(4) Where any provisions of the Scheme for Construction Contracts apply by virtue of this Part in default of contractual provision agreed by the parties, they have effect as implied terms of the contract concerned.

(5) Regulations under this section shall not be made unless a draft of them has been approved by resolution of each House of Parliament.

Service of notices, &c.

**115.**—(1) The parties are free to agree on the manner of service of any notice or other document required or authorised to be served in pursuance of the construction contract or for any of the purposes of this Part.

(2) If or to the extent that there is no such agreement the following provisions apply.

(3) A notice or other document may be served on a person by any effective means.

(4) If a notice or other document is addressed, pre-paid and delivered by post—

(a) to the addressee's last known principal residence or, if he is or has been carrying on a trade, profession or business, his last known principal business address, or

(b) where the addressee is a body corporate, to the body's registered or principal office,

it shall be treated as effectively served.

(5) This section does not apply to the service of documents for the purposes of legal proceedings, for which provision is made by rules of court.

(6) References in this Part to a notice or other document include any form of communication in writing and references to service shall be construed accordingly.

Reckoning periods of time.

**116.**—(1) For the purposes of this Part periods of time shall be reckoned as follows.

(2) Where an act is required to be done within a specified period after or from a specified date, the period begins immediately after that date.

1971 c. 80.

(3) Where the period would include Christmas Day, Good Friday or a day which under the Banking and Financial Dealings Act 1971 is a bank holiday in England and Wales or, as the case may be, in Scotland, that day shall be excluded.

Crown application.

**117.**—(1) This Part applies to a construction contract entered into by or on behalf of the Crown otherwise than by or on behalf of Her Majesty in her private capacity.

(2) This Part applies to a construction contract entered into on behalf of the Duchy of Cornwall notwithstanding any Crown interest.

(3)     Where a construction contract is entered into by or on behalf of Her Majesty in right of the Duchy of Lancaster, Her Majesty shall be represented, for the purposes of any adjudication or other proceedings arising out of the contract by virtue of this Part, by the Chancellor of the Duchy or such person as he may appoint.

(4)     Where a construction contract is entered into on behalf of the Duchy of Cornwall, the Duke of Cornwall or the possessor for the time being of the Duchy shall be represented, for the purposes of any adjudication or other proceedings arising out of the contract by virtue of this Part, by such person as he may appoint.

# Appendix C

# The Scheme for Construction Contracts (England and Wales) Regulations 1998 (SI No 649)

PART I

ADJUDICATION

**Notice of Intention to Seek Adjudication**

1.—(1) Any party to a construction contract (the "referring party") may give written notice (the "notice of adjudication") of his intention to refer any dispute arising under the contract, to adjudication.

(2) The notice of adjudication shall be given to every other party to the contract.

(3) The notice of adjudication shall set out briefly—

(a) the nature and a brief description of the dispute and of the parties involved,

(b) details of where and when the dispute has arisen,

(c) the nature of the redress which is sought, and

(d) the names and addresses of the parties to the contract (including, where appropriate, the addresses which the parties have specified for the giving of notices).

2.—(1) Following the giving of a notice of adjudication and subject to any agreement between the parties to the dispute as to who shall act as adjudicator—

(a) the referring party shall request the person (if any) specified in the contract to act as adjudicator, or

(b) if no person is named in the contract or the person named has already indicated that he is unwilling or unable to act, and the contract provides for a specified nominating body to select a person, the referring party shall request the nominating body named in the contract to select a person to act as adjudicator, or

(c) where neither paragraph (a) nor (b) above applies, or where the person referred to in (a) has already indicated that he is unwilling or unable to act and (b) does not apply, the referring party shall request an adjudicator nominating body to select a person to act as adjudicator.

(2) A person requested to act as adjudicator in accordance with the provisions of paragraph (1) shall indicate whether or not he is willing to act within two days of receiving the request.

(3) In this paragraph, and in paragraphs 5 and 6 below, an "adjudicator nominating body" shall mean a body (not being a natural person and not being a party to the dispute) which holds itself out publicly as a body which will select an adjudicator when requested to do so by a referring party.

3. The request referred to in paragraphs 2, 5 and 6 shall be accompanied by a copy of the notice of adjudication.

4. Any person requested or selected to act as adjudicator in accordance with paragraphs 2, 5 or 6 shall be a natural person acting in his personal capacity. A person requested or selected to act as

an adjudicator shall not be an employee of any of the parties to the dispute and shall declare any interest, financial or otherwise, in any matter relating to the dispute.

5.—(1) The nominating body referred to in paragraphs 2(1)(b) and 6(1)(b) or the adjudicator nominating body referred to in paragraphs 2(1)(c), 5(2)(b) and 6(1)(c) must communicate the selection of an adjudicator to the referring party within five days of receiving a request to do so.

(2) Where the nominating body or the adjudicator nominating body fails to comply with paragraph (1), the referring party may—

(a) agree with the other party to the dispute to request a specified person to act as adjudicator, or

(b) request any other adjudicator nominating body to select a person to act as adjudicator.

(3) The person requested to act as adjudicator in accordance with the provisions of paragraphs (1) or (2) shall indicate whether or not he is willing to act within two days of receiving the request.

6.—(1) Where an adjudicator who is named in the contract indicates to the parties that he is unable or unwilling to act, or where he fails to respond in accordance with paragraph 2(2), the referring party may—

(a) request another person (if any) specified in the contract to act as adjudicator, or

(b) request the nominating body (if any) referred to in the contract to select a person to act as adjudicator, or

(c) request any other adjudicator nominating body to select a person to act as adjudicator.

(2) The person requested to act in accordance with the provisions of paragraph (1) shall indicate whether or not he is willing to act within two days of receiving the request.

7.—(1) Where an adjudicator has been selected in accordance with paragraphs 2, 5 or 6, the referring party shall, not later than seven days from the date of the notice of adjudication, refer the dispute in writing (the "referral notice") to the adjudicator.

(2) A referral notice shall be accompanied by copies of, or relevant extracts from, the construction contract and such other documents as the referring party intends to rely upon.

(3) The referring party shall, at the same time as he sends to the adjudicator the documents referred to in paragraphs (1) and (2), send copies of those documents to every other party to the dispute.

8.—(1) The adjudicator may, with the consent of all the parties to those disputes, adjudicate at the same time on more than one dispute under the same contract.

(2) The adjudicator may, with the consent of all the parties to those disputes, adjudicate at the same time on related disputes under different contracts, whether or not one or more of those parties is a party to those disputes.

(3) All the parties in paragraphs (1) and (2) respectively may agree to extend the period within which the adjudicator may reach a decision in relation to all or any of these disputes.

(4) Where an adjudicator ceases to act because a dispute is to be adjudicated on by another person in terms of this paragraph, that adjudicator's fees and expenses shall be determined in accordance with paragraph 25.

9.—(1) An adjudicator may resign at any time on giving notice in writing to the parties to the dispute.

(2) An adjudicator must resign where the dispute is the same or substantially the same as one which has previously been referred to adjudication, and a decision has been taken in that adjudication.

(3) Where an adjudicator ceases to act under paragraph 9(1)—

(a) the referring party may serve a fresh notice under paragraph 1 and shall request an adjudicator to act in accordance with paragraphs 2 to 7; and

(b) if requested by the new adjudicator and insofar as it is reasonably practicable, the parties shall supply him with copies of all documents which they had made available to the previous adjudicator.

(4) Where an adjudicator resigns in the circumstances referred to in paragraph (2), or where a dispute varies significantly from the dispute referred to him in the referral notice and for that reason he is not competent to decide it, the adjudicator shall be entitled to the payment of such reasonable amount as he may determine by way of fees and expenses reasonably incurred by him. The parties shall be jointly and severally liable for any sum which remains outstanding following the making of any determination on how the payment shall be apportioned.

10. Where any party to the dispute objects to the appointment of a particular person as adjudicator, that objection shall not invalidate the adjudicator's appointment nor any decision he

may reach in accordance with paragraph 20.

**11.**—(1) The parties to a dispute may at any time agree to revoke the appointment of the adjudicator. The adjudicator shall be entitled to the payment of such reasonable amount as he may determine by way of fees and expenses incurred by him. The parties shall be jointly and severally liable for any sum which remains outstanding following the making of any determination on how the payment shall be apportioned.

(2) Where the revocation of the appointment of the adjudicator is due to the default or misconduct of the adjudicator, the parties shall not be liable to pay the adjudicator's fees and expenses.

### Powers of the adjudicator

**12.** The adjudicator shall—

(a) act impartially in carrying out his duties and shall do so in accordance with any relevant terms of the contract and shall reach his decision in accordance with the applicable law in relation to the contract; and

(b) avoid incurring unnecessary expense.

**13.** The adjudicator may take the initiative in ascertaining the facts and the law necessary to determine the dispute, and shall decide on the procedure to be followed in the adjudication. In particular he may—

(a) request any party to the contract to supply him with such documents as he may reasonably require including, if he so directs, any written statement from any party to the contract supporting or supplementing the referral notice and any other documents given under paragraph 7(2),

(b) decide the language or languages to be used in the adjudication and whether a translation of any document is to be provided and if so by whom,

(c) meet and question any of the parties to the contract and their representatives,

(d) subject to obtaining any necessary consent from a third party or parties, make such site visits and inspections as he considers appropriate, whether accompanied by the parties or not,

(e) subject to obtaining any necessary consent from a third party or parties, carry out any tests or experiments,

(f) obtain and consider such representations and submissions as he requires, and, provided he has notified the parties of his intention, appoint experts, assessors or legal advisers,

(g) give directions as to the timetable for the adjudication, any deadlines, or limits as to the length of written documents or oral representations to be complied with, and

(h) issue other directions relating to the conduct of the adjudication.

**14.** The parties shall comply with any request or direction of the adjudicator in relation to the adjudication.

**15.** If, without showing sufficient cause, a party fails to comply with any request, direction or timetable of the adjudicator made in accordance with his powers, fails to produce any document or written statement requested by the adjudicator, or in any other way fails to comply with a requirement under these provisions relating to the adjudication, the adjudicator may—

(a) continue the adjudication in the absence of that party or of the document or written statement requested,

(b) draw such inferences from that failure to comply as circumstances may, in the adjudicator's opinion, be justified, and

(c) make a decision on the basis of the information before him attaching such weight as he thinks fit to any evidence submitted to him outside any period he may have requested or directed.

**16.**—(1) Subject to any agreement between the parties to the contrary, and to the terms of paragraph (2) below, any party to the dispute may be assisted by, or represented by, such advisers or representatives (whether legally qualified or not) as he considers appropriate.

(2) Where the adjudicator is considering oral evidence or representations, a party to the dispute may not be represented by more than one person, unless the adjudicator gives directions to the contrary.

**17.** The adjudicator shall consider any relevant information submitted to him by any of the parties to the dispute and shall make available to them any information to be taken into account in reaching his decision.

**18.** The adjudicator and any party to the dispute shall not disclose to any other person any information or document provided to him in connection with the adjudication which the party supplying it has indicated is to be treated as confidential, except to the extent that it is necessary for the purposes of, or in connection with, the adjudication.

**19.**—(1) The adjudicator shall reach his decision not later than—

(a) twenty eight days after the date of the referral notice mentioned in paragraph 7(1), or

(b) forty two days after the date of the referral notice if the referring party so consents, or

(c) such period exceeding twenty eight days after the referral notice as the parties to the dispute may, after the giving of that notice, agree.

(2) Where the adjudicator fails, for any reason, to reach his decision in accordance with paragraph (1)

(a) any of the parties to the dispute may serve a fresh notice under paragraph 1 and shall request an adjudicator to act in accordance with paragraphs 2 to 7; and

(b) if requested by the new adjudicator and insofar as it is reasonably practicable, the parties shall supply him with copies of all documents which they had made available to the previous adjudicator.

(3) As soon as possible after he has reached a decision, the adjudicator shall deliver a copy of that decision to each of the parties to the contract.

### Adjudicator's decision

**20.** The adjudicator shall decide the matters in dispute. He may take into account any other matters which the parties to the dispute agree should be within the scope of the adjudication or which are matters under the contract which he considers are necessarily connected with the dispute. In particular, he may—

(a) open up, revise and review any decision taken or any certificate given by any person referred to in the contract unless the contract states that the decision or certificate is final and conclusive,

(b) decide that any of the parties to the dispute is liable to make a payment under the contract (whether in sterling or some other currency) and, subject to section 111(4) of the Act, when that payment is due and the final date for payment,

(c) having regard to any term of the contract relating to the payment of interest decide the circumstances in which, and the rates at which, and the periods for which simple or compound rates of interest shall be paid.

**21.** In the absence of any directions by the adjudicator relating to the time for performance of his decision, the parties shall be required to comply with any decision of the adjudicator immediately on delivery of the decision to the parties in accordance with this paragraph.

**22.** If requested by one of the parties to the dispute, the adjudicator shall provide reasons for his decision.

Effects of the decision

**23.**—(1) In his decision, the adjudicator may, if he thinks fit, order any of the parties to comply peremptorily with his decision or any part of it.

(2) The decision of the adjudicator shall be binding on the parties, and they shall comply with it until the dispute is finally determined by legal proceedings, by arbitration (if the contract provides for arbitration or the parties otherwise agree to arbitration) or by agreement between the parties.

**24.** Section 42 of the Arbitration Act 1996 shall apply to this Scheme subject to the following modifications—

(a) in subsection (2) for the word "tribunal" wherever it appears there shall be substituted the word "adjudicator",

(b) in subparagraph (b) of subsection (2) for the words "arbitral proceedings" there shall be substituted the word "adjudication",

(c) subparagraph (c) of subsection (2) shall be deleted, and

(d) subsection (3) shall be deleted.

**25.** The adjudicator shall be entitled to the payment of such reasonable amount as he may determine by way of fees and expenses reasonably incurred by him. The parties shall be jointly and severally liable for any sum which remains outstanding following the making of any determination on how the payment shall be apportioned.

**26.** The adjudicator shall not be liable for anything done or omitted in the discharge or purported discharge of his functions as adjudicator unless the act or omission is in bad faith, and any employee or agent of the adjudicator shall be similarly protected from liability.

PART II

PAYMENT

### Entitlement to and amount of stage payments

**1.** Where the parties to a relevant construction contract fail to agree—

(a) the amount of any instalment or stage or periodic payment for any work under the contract, or

(b) the intervals at which, or circumstances in which, such payments become due under that contract, or

(c) both of the matters mentioned in sub-paragraphs (a) and (b) above,

the relevant provisions of paragraphs 2 to 4 below shall apply.

**2.**—(1) The amount of any payment by way of instalments or stage or periodic payments in respect of a relevant period shall be the difference between the amount determined in accordance with sub-paragraph (2) and the amount determined in accordance with sub-paragraph (3).

(2) The aggregate of the following amounts—

(a) an amount equal to the value of any work performed in accordance with the relevant construction contract during the period from the commencement of the contract to the end of the relevant period (excluding any amount calculated in accordance with sub-paragraph (b)),

(b) where the contract provides for payment for materials, an amount equal to the value of any materials manufactured on site or brought onto site for the purposes of the works during the period from the commencement of the contract to the end of the relevant period, and

(c) any other amount or sum which the contract specifies shall be payable during or in respect of the period from the commencement of the contract to the end of the relevant period.

(3) The aggregate of any sums which have been paid or are due for payment by way of instalments, stage or periodic payments during the period from the commencement of the contract to the end of the relevant period.

(4) An amount calculated in accordance with this paragraph shall not exceed the difference between—

(a) the contract price, and

(b) the aggregate of the instalments or stage or periodic payments which have become due.

### Dates for payment

**3.** Where the parties to a construction contract fail to provide an adequate mechanism for determining either what payments become due under the contract, or when they become due for payment, or both, the relevant provisions of paragraphs 4 to 7 shall apply.

**4.** Any payment of a kind mentioned in paragraph 2 above shall become due on whichever of the following dates occurs later—

(a) the expiry of 7 days following the relevant period mentioned in paragraph 2(1) above, or

(b) the making of a claim by the payee.

**5.** The final payment payable under a relevant construction contract, namely the payment of an amount equal to the difference (if any) between—

(a) the contract price, and

(b) the aggregate of any instalment or stage or periodic payments which have become due under the contract,

shall become due on the expiry of—

(a) 30 days following completion of the work, or

(b) the making of a claim by the payee,

whichever is the later.

**6.** Payment of the contract price under a construction contract (not being a relevant construc-

tion contract) shall become due on
  (a) the expiry of 30 days following the completion of the work, or
  (b) the making of a claim by the payee,
whichever is the later.
  7. Any other payment under a construction contract shall become due
  (a) on the expiry of 7 days following the completion of the work to which the payment
  relates, or
  (b) the making of a claim by the payee,
whichever is the later.

### Final date for payment

8.—(1) Where the parties to a construction contract fail to provide a final date for payment in
relation to any sum which becomes due under a construction contract, the provisions of this
paragraph shall apply.
  (2) The final date for the making of any payment of a kind mentioned in paragraphs 2, 5, 6 or
7, shall be 17 days from the date that payment becomes due.

### Notice specifying amount of payment

9. A party to a construction contract shall, not later than 5 days after the date on which any
payment—
  (a) becomes due from him, or
  (b) would have become due, if—
      (i) the other party had carried out his obligations under the contract, and
      (ii) no set—off or abatement was permitted by reference to any sum claimed to be due
      . under one or more other contracts,
give notice to the other party to the contract specifying the amount (if any) of the payment he has
made or proposes to make, specifying to what the payment relates and the basis on which that
amount is calculated.

### Notice of intention to withhold payment

10. Any notice of intention to withhold payment mentioned in section 111 of the Act shall be
given not later than the prescribed period, which is to say not later than 7 days before the final
date for payment determined either in accordance with the construction contract, or where no
such provision is made in the contract, in accordance with paragraph 8 above.

### Prohibition of conditional payment provisions

11. Where a provision making payment under a construction contract conditional on the payer
receiving payment from a third person is ineffective as mentioned in section 113 of the Act, and
the parties have not agreed other terms for payment, the relevant provisions of—
  (a) paragraphs 2, 4, 5, 7, 8, 9 and 10 shall apply in the case of a relevant construction
  contract, and
  (b) paragraphs 6, 7, 8, 9 and 10 shall apply in the case of any other construction contract.

### Interpretation

12. In this Part of the Scheme for Construction Contracts—
  "claim by the payee" means a written notice given by the party carrying out work under a
  construction contract to the other party specifying the amount of any payment or payments
  which he considers to be due and the basis on which it is, or they are calculated;
  "contract price" means the entire sum payable under the construction contract in respect of
  the work;
  "relevant construction contract" means any construction contract other than one—
  (a) which specifies that the duration of the work is to be less than 45 days, or
  (b) in respect of which the parties agree that the duration of the work is estimated to be less
  than 45 days;
  "relevant period" means a period which is specified in, or is calculated by reference to the
  construction contract or where no such period is so specified or is so calculable, a period of
  28 days;

"value of work" means an amount determined in accordance with the construction contract under which the work is performed or where the contract contains no such provision, the cost of any work performed in accordance with that contract together with an amount equal to any overhead or profit included in the contract price;

"work" means any of the work or services mentioned in section 104 of the Act.

# Appendix D

# The Construction Contracts (England and Wales) Exclusion Order 1998 (SI No 648)

### Citation, commencement and extent

**1.**—(1) This Order may be cited as the Construction Contracts (England and Wales) Exclusion Order 1998 and shall come into force at the end of the period of 8 weeks beginning with the day on which it is made ("the commencement date").

(2) This Order shall extend to England and Wales only.

### Interpretation

**2.** In this Order, "Part II" means Part II of the Housing Grants, Construction and Regeneration Act 1996.

### Agreements under statute

**3.** A construction contract is excluded from the operation of Part II if it is—

(a) an agreement under section 38 (power of highway authorities to adopt by agreement) or section 278 (agreements as to execution of works) of the Highways Act 1980[2];

(b) an agreement under section 106 (planning obligations), 106A (modification or discharge of planning obligations) or 299A (Crown planning obligations) of the Town and Country Planning Act 1990[3];

(c) an agreement under section 104 of the Water Industry Act 1991[4] (agreements to adopt sewer, drain or sewage disposal works); or

(d) an externally financed development agreement within the meaning of section 1 of the National Health Service (Private Finance) Act 1997[5] (powers of NHS Trusts to enter into agreements).

### Private finance initiative

**4.**—(1) A construction contract is excluded from the operation of Part II if it is a contract entered into under the private finance initiative, within the meaning given below.

(2) A contract is entered into under the private finance initiative if all the following conditions are fulfilled—

(a) it contains a statement that it is entered into under that initiative or, as the case may be, under a project applying similar principles;

(b) the consideration due under the contract is determined at least in part by reference to one or more of the following—

    (i) the standards attained in the performance of a service, the provision of which is the principal purpose or one of the principal purposes for which the building or structure is constructed;

      (ii)  the extent, rate or intensity of use of all or any part of the building or structure in question; or

      (iii) the right to operate any facility in connection with the building or structure in question; and

  (c) one of the parties to the contract is—

      (i)   a Minister of the Crown;

      (ii)  a department in respect of which appropriation accounts are required to be prepared under the Exchequer and Audit Departments Act 1866[6];

      (iii) any other authority or body whose accounts are required to be examined and certified by or are open to the inspection of the Comptroller and Auditor General by virtue of an agreement entered into before the commencement date or by virtue of any enactment;

      (iv) any authority or body listed in Schedule 4 to the National Audit Act 1983[7] (nationalised industries and other public authorities);

      (v)  a body whose accounts are subject to audit by auditors appointed by the Audit Commission;

      (vi) the governing body or trustees of a voluntary school within the meaning of section 31 of the Education Act 1996[8] (county schools and voluntary schools), or

      (vii) a company wholly owned by any of the bodies described in paragraphs (i) to (v).

### Finance agreements

**5.**—(1) A construction contract is excluded from the operation of Part II if it is a finance agreement, within the meaning given below.

  (2) A contract is a finance agreement if it is any one of the following—

  (a) any contract of insurance;

  (b) any contract under which the principal obligations include the formation or dissolution of a company, unincorporated association or partnership;

  (c) any contract under which the principal obligations include the creation or transfer of securities or any right or interest in securities;

  (d) any contract under which the principal obligations include the lending of money;

  (e) any contract under which the principal obligations include an undertaking by a person to be responsible as surety for the debt or default of another person, including a fidelity bond, advance payment bond, retention bond or performance bond.

### Development agreements

**6.**—(1) A construction contract is excluded from the operation of Part II if it is a development agreement, within the meaning given below.

  (2) A contract is a development agreement if it includes provision for the grant or disposal of a relevant interest in the land on which take place the principal construction operations to which the contract relates.

  (3) In paragraph (2) above, a relevant interest in land means—

  (a) a freehold; or

  (b) a leasehold for a period which is to expire no earlier than 12 months after the completion of the construction operations under the contract.